LEARN TO QUILT

LEARN
TO
QUILT

SHARON CHAMBERS

This paperback edition first published in 2008 by
New Holland Publishers (UK) Ltd
London · Cape Town · Sydney · Auckland

Garfield House, 86–88 Edgware Road
London W2 2EA
United Kingdom
www.newhollandpublishers.com

80 McKenzie Street
Cape Town 8001
South Africa

Unit 1, 66 Gibbes Street
Chatswood
NSW 2067
Australia

218 Lake Road
Northcote, Auckland
New Zealand

ISBN 978 1 84773 227 9

Senior Editor: Clare Sayer
Production: Hazel Kirkman
Design: Frances de Rees
Photographer: Shona Wood
Illustrations: Carrie Hill
Editorial Direction: Rosemary Wilkinson

1 3 5 7 9 10 8 6 4 2

Reproduction by Pica Digital PTE Ltd, Singapore
Printed and bound by Times Offset (M) Sdn. Bhd., Malaysia

CONTENTS

INTRODUCTION

One of the aspects of my job running workshops on quiltmaking that has given me the most pleasure over the years, is observing the students progress from hesitant beginner to confident quilter. The quilts they make are as different as the quilters are – extrovert, calm, country cosy or city smart. But all of us share a desire that links us to people throughout the ages, the need to make beautiful, useful and decorative objects with our own hands.

The great news is that it couldn't be easier, and this book is here to show you how. The chapters that follow take you from a simple handmade cot quilt to an ingenious throw masquerading as a cushion. You will learn, in easy stages, how to use rotary cutting equipment and quick piecing strategies, but traditional techniques are not forgotten either.

Throughout the book I have tried to offer you helpful tips gleaned from my twenty-plus years of experience. By that I do not mean to imply that I am an "expert". I still make mistakes, just different ones now, and usually more complicated to correct. But it is the quiet satisfaction of working with my hands in such a tactile craft, and the joy of seeing an idea made real in beautiful fabrics and textured stitches, that has kept me quilting through thick and thin.

It is a journey of discovery; some of us are just a little bit further along the road than others. So consider this book your traveller's guide and wave to me as you go past. Happy quilting, and may you never have to unpick a stitch!

Sharon Chambers

Basic Information

Patchwork is easily accessible to all who wish to try it. Centuries of quilters have found a creative outlet using only their imagination, the simplest of tools and some scraps of fabric.

FABRICS

Traditionally quilts were made from old pieces of clothing and soft furnishings. Choose fabrics that are 100% cotton as these tightly-woven, smooth fabrics are much easier to work with, especially for beginners. Also, all fabrics used in a project should be of a similar weight. You may decide to wash all your fabrics before using but it is always a good idea to test each one for colourfastness. Fabrics should be washed in cool to tepid water using a mild non-enzyme detergent which contains no bleach or optical whiteners. Press the fabric while it is still damp.

Unless otherwise stated any ¼ yard/25 cm requirement is the "long" quarter (the full width of the fabric) and not the "fat" quarter, which is a piece 18 x 22 in (50 x 56 cm).

THREADS

Purchase good-quality sewing thread. I usually buy large reels of cotton thread in a limited range of neutral colours (off-white, mid-grey, beige and black), for all my hand and machine piecing. Use a colour that won't show through the lightest fabric you are using. For hand quilting there are cotton and cotton-wrapped polyester threads, most with a glaze on them to reduce friction when drawing the thread through the quilt layers. There is also an extremely fine nylon thread for "invisible" machine quilting. Heavier threads such as coton à broder are used for tying and naive-style quilting.

SCISSORS

Invest in a large, sharp pair of scissors for cutting fabric. And only use them for fabric. Downgrade your old pair and keep them for cutting paper and card. A small, sharp pair of needlework scissors would be useful too.

NEEDLES

You will need a selection of needles in an assortment of sizes: sharps for hand piecing and finishing, betweens for quilting, a Japanese Sashiko needle or a large-eye embroidery needle for big stitch quilting and/or tying using the thicker threads, and finally, machine needles.

NOTE:
If you have trouble threading your needle, use a hands-free magnifying glass and thread a whole packet of needles onto the reel of thread at once; then you only have to pull off each needle with a length of thread as you need it.

MARKERS

Fabric markers are used for marking stitching and quilting lines on light and dark fabrics. Some specialist pencils have lead designed for use on fabrics and produce a very fine line. A Hera marker is a useful spatula-shaped tool which you can use to press a shiny crease line onto the fabric. Because there is no colour involved, it works equally well on light, dark or heavily-patterned fabrics. Permanent pens in black or selected colours are used to write quilt labels. The ink should be acid-free and of archival quality so as not to rot the fabric over time.

SEWING KIT

Your sewing kit should include straight pins and safety pins, size 1. A seam ripper is useful for the inevitable mistakes. It is also invaluable, when held flat side against the fabric, for holding patches firmly in place while stitching. Use it as a safer alternative to your fingers for guiding fabric underneath the presser foot of your machine. Another essential item is a thimble. I've tried almost every kind available but keep coming back to the same old standby – a cheap, ordinary metal thimble that fits perfectly and feels comfortable. I use mine on the middle finger of my dominant hand to push the needle through the fabric. When quilting in a hoop I also use a raised-edge quilter's thimble on the hand underneath. You'll find thimbles made of leather or plastic or fabric while others have openings for long fingernails or wrap around your finger like a bandage.

Your sewing machine is an essential piece of equipment and machine quilting certainly speeds up the whole process. You will also probably need a walking foot attachment. To get the best from your machine, make sure you have it serviced regularly.

ROTARY CUTTING EQUIPMENT

Almost everything mentioned so far has been a fairly standard component of any good sewing box. The truly innovative items of the last few decades must surely be rotary cutting equipment. The rotary cutter is a sharp circular knife which is used in conjunction with a thick plastic ruler (never wood or metal) and a self-healing cutting mat to measure and then cut patches directly from fabric, several layers at a time, if desired. The patches are much more accurate than those which are produced using a traditional template. They are also cut with minimum effort on your part and with minimum wastage. There are different sizes of cutters and mats – the size of the cutter and mat is up to you; most people prefer the 45 mm (1¾ in) blade and the medium size mat.

BELOW, clockwise from left: cutting mat, Hera marker, rotary cutter, embroidery thread, quilting hoop, needles, rotary ruler, fabric markers, dressmaking pins, quilter's quarter, seam ripper, scissors, thimble, sewing thread.

When using a rotary cutter, you need a good acrylic ruler, ideally one which has the measurements marked in both directions. Choose a long, wide one, but if you enjoy making quilts, as I hope you will, a smaller one plus a square will come in very handy. They are an expensive investment, but worth every penny. A quilter's quarter is a handy tool for marking your seam allowances as it is exactly ¼ in (0.75 cm) thick.

WORK TABLE

Although, technically, not part of your sewing kit, the table and chair you use deserve a mention here. Work at a table that is the right height for you. Choose a comfortable chair, perhaps an adjustable one, that offers good support for your back and legs. An adjustable work light is invaluable. Position it where it won't cast shadows on your work. You can buy daylight-simulation bulbs which many quilters prefer, especially for colour work.

Remember to gently stretch your back and neck muscles from time to time, thus relieving any tension. Flex your arms and hands. Get up from your chair regularly to keep the circulation in your legs moving.

This equipment list is by no means exhaustive or imperative. The items are all things that I have found useful or that my quilting friends and colleagues use and recommend. Start with the basics and add to your supplies as and when you need them. Think about your own personal likes and dislikes when choosing equipment or gadgets.

NOTES ON MEASUREMENTS

Both imperial and metric measurements are given for purchasing fabrics as well as cutting and stitching each project. These measurements are not interchangeable. I have tried to keep the same proportions for each set of measurements, but some variation is inevitable.

When calculating amounts of fabric to purchase, I have aimed to err on the side of generosity to allow some leeway for mistakes or cutting extra patches, however, I have also assumed that you will try to be as careful as possible. Any leftover pieces of fabric may be saved and used for small projects or in a simple scrap quilt.

Unless otherwise stated, all seam allowances are ¼ in for imperial and 0.75 cm for metric.

SAFETY NOTES
- **Always follow sensible safety precautions when using rotary cutting equipment and store securely, well out of the reach of children and pets.**
- **Always cover the blade with the built-in safety guard as soon as you finish cutting and every time you lay the cutter down.**
- **Always make a single slow cut away from your body. Do not draw the blade back towards yourself. Do not cut from extreme right to extreme left (or vice-versa if left-handed) across in front of yourself.**
- **Always use the special heavy-gauge plastic rotary rulers, not wooden or metal ones which quickly dull your blade.**
- **Always use the special self-healing cutting mat.**
- **Always use fabric adhesive sprays in well-ventilated rooms away from naked flames.**
- **Take regular breaks from repetitive tasks so you don't cause strain or injury to your muscles and tendons.**
- **Ensure your working area is properly lit and that tables, chairs and ironing boards are at the correct height and position for your requirements.**

THE ELEMENTS OF A QUILT

Binding

Outer border

Inner border

Straight setting

On point setting

Corner triangle

Backing

Straight corner

Wadding

Outline quilting

Setting triangle

Pieced block

Grid quilting

Sashing strip

Mitred corner

Alternate block

CARE AND STORAGE OF QUILTS

Some quilters prefer to prewash all fabrics; others prefer to work with fabric that retains its factory finish. It is always a good idea to test a small square of each fabric you intend to use for colour-fastness.

Wash finished quilts in cool (never hot) water using a simple mild detergent which does not contain enzymes, phosphates, bleach or optical whiteners. If in doubt, use a clear washing-up liquid detergent whose main ingredient is labelled as "non-ionic surfactant".

If using a machine, wash on the wool setting with the gentlest possible spin cycle. If washing by hand in the bathtub, do not wring or twist the quilt. Rinse carefully and thoroughly, letting the water drain away completely before gently pressing excess water out. It will be very heavy so enlist help to lift the quilt. Support the wet quilt at all times so as not to cause a strain on the threads.

Dry the quilt flat, preferably outside. Spread it out on the ground over a large sheet, in dappled shade if possible. Cover with another sheet to protect from sunlight. Choose a dry, breezy day. Turn the quilt over to finish drying the other side.

Protect quilts from the damaging effects of direct sunlight.

Fold quilts with the right side out, padding the folds with acid-free tissue to protect from creases.

Do not store on bare wood which can cause staining. Paint or seal the wood, and line the shelf with several layers of acid-free tissue as well.

Air your quilt, re-fold it along different lines and renew the tissue at least once a year. You can store a quilt wrapped in a clean sheet or pillowcase for extra protection, but refrain from using plastic bags which don't allow the air to circulate.

Basic Quilting Techniques

Discover one of life's simple pleasures. Quilting is inexpensive, eco-friendly and portable. The following techniques show you how to make a simple hand pieced quilt.

MAKING TEMPLATES FOR HAND PIECING

Templates for hand piecing are cut to the exact size of the finished patch and are used to mark the stitching lines. The seam allowances are added when the fabric shapes are being cut.

You will often be given template shapes ready to trace, but most blocks are simple to draw using squared paper, a ruler and a pencil. The shapes are cut from template plastic. Generally blocks are based on a grid. Patterns are grouped according to the type of grid which defines their construction, such as four-patch (see Happy Days Quilt, page 14).

Work on a self-healing cutting mat. Make sure the plastic sheet is at room temperature (to make it more pliable) and tape the plastic sheet over the template shape using low-tack masking tape. Place the edge of a ruler precisely over one of the lines, and holding it firmly in place, use a craft knife to score along the line starting and finishing about $\frac{1}{4}$ in (0.75 cm) longer than the line you are copying. This ensures sharp corners with no "hangnails". When all sides have been scored, gently bend the plastic back and forth until you can release the template. Mark with the name and size of the block. You may also need a grain line arrow to indicate the direction of placement on the fabric **(A)**.

A

MARKING AND CUTTING OUT PATCHES

Lay out your fabric, right side down, on a hard flat surface. Place the template on the fabric with the grain line arrow in line with either the lengthways or crossways threads, but avoiding the selvedges. Holding the template firmly in place, draw around it with a pencil suitable for your fabric. This is the stitching line. Remove the template, and using a rotary ruler or a quilter's quarter, mark a second line $\frac{1}{4}$ in (0.75 cm) outside the first. This is the cutting line. Continue until you have marked as many patches as you need from that fabric. For economy, nest the patches closely together **(B)**.

B

Using sharp scissors, cut carefully around each shape along the cutting lines. Mark and cut all the patches from each fabric in the same way.

You may want to put everything for one block in a separate envelope along with a needle, thread and scissors so you can work on your block in snatched moments.

HAND PIECING

Patchwork blocks are put together in a logical manner, stitching the smallest pieces together first and stitching in straight lines wherever

possible. All seam allowances are left unstitched. Use a single length of thread in a colour to blend with your fabrics. Cut it about 18 in (45 cm) long and place a knot in the end you have just cut. Thread a sharps sewing needle with the other end.

Lay out all the patches as they will appear in the finished block **(C)**. Pick up the first two patches, place them right sides together and pin the seam lines at the beginning, the end

C

and as many as you need in the middle. The seam lines on each fabric should line up exactly. When you put the pin in, turn the patches over to check that the pin emerges on the seam line at the back. Start stitching at the corner with a knot and a backstitch **(diagram 1)**.

DIAGRAM 1

Then take running stitches with a back stitch every once in a while for strength, say, every five to ten stitches depending on how small your stitches are **(D)**. Finish off the seam with a backstitch and a knot.

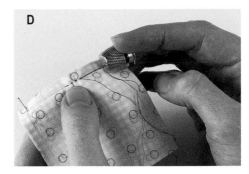

D

When stitching intersecting seams, take a backstitch approaching the intersection, take your needle through the junction and backstitch on the other side as you emerge (**E**). These are potential weak spots, and backstitching helps to keep them from stretching or breaking.

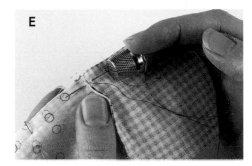

E

Do not press until you have finished the whole block. Press the seams to one side: usually towards the darker fabric. Where multiple patches join, you may have to press the seams in a circular fashion.

When all the blocks are complete, lay them out in their final positions. Stitch the blocks together in strips, and then stitch the long strips together, matching and pinning where the short seams intersect.

SIMPLE BIG STITCH QUILTING

This is a very quick simplified version of the normal quilting process. The naive quality of such large stitches works well on children's quilts and on any project where you want a country style or folk art look. Although some quilters may disagree, I suggest you try quilting first of all without a hoop. When you do try a hoop later you will have some knowledge on which to base your comparison.

Choose a thicker quilting thread such as coton à broder no. 16 or a fine perlé cotton. The choice of colour is up to you although a slightly darker shade increases the illusion of depth. Use a large size betweens needle, embroidery needle or a Sashiko needle. Now is a good time to start using a thimble. Most people learn to use one eventually, at least on the finger that pushes the needle.

At this point the pieced top is added to a backing fabric with wadding sandwiched between. Prepare your backing fabric, piecing lengths together if necessary. Remove your wadding from its packaging and allow it to absorb moisture from the atmosphere to release the wrinkles. The longer you leave it, the better. The three layers need to be held together temporarily, while they are quilted either by hand or machine.

For speed, instead of holding the three layers (called the quilt "sandwich") together with large tacking stitches, you can use fabric spray adhesive to stick them together. Make sure you follow the instructions on the spray can. Choose a large flat surface in a well-ventilated room and protect the surrounding area with scrap fabric or paper. Spread out the wadding so there are no wrinkles. Spray the surface according to the directions on the can. Centre the backing fabric on the wadding, right side up. The adhesive is not permanent so you can lift the fabric and reposition it if you need to. Turn the backed wadding over, spray it on the other side as before and place the quilt centrally on top, right side up. Make sure there are no wrinkles on either the back or the front. Place a few safety pins in the quilt just for insurance.

Using a Hera marker and a long quilter's ruler, mark diagonal quilting lines by pressing firmly with the marker and sliding it along the edge of the ruler.

Thread your needle with a long (18–20 in/45–50 cm) single length of coton à broder knotted at one end. Insert the needle into one of the quilting lines, about 1 in (2.5 cm) from where the line ends. Push the needle into the quilt and wadding only, bring the needle out at the end of the quilting line

and pull on it firmly until the knot pops into and lodges inside the wadding. As you quilt back over this tail you will secure it even further (**diagram 2**).

DIAGRAM 2

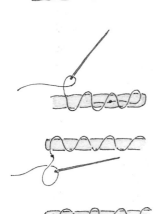

You may find it easier to hold the quilt in your lap while working or spread it out on a table. The hand underneath the quilt holds it by gathering up a small pleat of the quilt sandwich and pushing upwards at the point of the stitch while the needle is being directed downwards. Push the needle straight down through all three layers until you can just feel it exit at the back. As soon as the point of the needle gently touches your finger, it is deflected back upwards to form the stitch (see page 42). For this naive-style quilting, your stitches, and the spaces between, should be about $\frac{1}{4}$ in (0.75 cm) long. You will soon find the rhythm that suits you. Aim to put enough tension on the thread to slightly compress the layers but do not pull the thread so tight that gathers appear. Too loose is better than too tight. When you wish to fasten off, take the last stitch straight through to the back of the quilt and put a knot in the thread about $\frac{1}{4}$ in (0.75 cm) away from the quilt surface. Taking a tiny backstitch, push the needle into the quilt and wadding (do not come through to the front), tug on it again and hide the knot inside (**diagram 2**). Trim off the thread even with the back of the quilt.

"Happy Days" Quilt

This traditional hand-pieced patchwork is made from two sizes of squares with very simple quilting holding the layers together. The edges are turned in with a rickrack insertion. The size of the project means it can be quickly finished.

Finished size: 25 x 35 in (65 x 91 cm)

MATERIALS

All fabrics are 45 in (115 cm) wide, 100% cotton

Large squares: bright floral fabric, ⅔ yd (60 cm)

Four-patch blocks: two brightly contrasting fabrics, ½ yd (40 cm) each

Backing: co-ordinating small print, 29 x 39 in (75 x 100 cm)

Wadding: 100% cotton, 29 x 39 in (75 x 100 cm)

Edges: bright coloured rick rack, 3⅝ yds (3.3 m)

Thread: coton à broder no. 16, 1 skein

A4 sheet of template plastic, ruler, craft knife, masking tape

Markers: permanent pen for marking on plastic, fabric marking pencil that will be visible on your fabrics, Hera marker

Needles: sharps sewing needle, Sashiko or large quilting needle

Quilter's quarter

Saucer or small round plate

Fabric spray adhesive

PREPARATION

1 Using the A4 template plastic, a ruler and craft knife, prepare templates A and B from the patterns on page 91, choosing either the imperial or the metric set.

2 Wash and press your fabrics. Open the wadding and let it breathe.

3 On the back of the bright floral fabric, mark out eighteen large squares using template A. On the back of each of the two contrasting fabrics, mark out thirty-four small squares using template B. Using a rotary ruler, mark the cutting lines ¼ in (0.75 cm) outside the stitching lines.

NOTE:
If your template slips while drawing around it, try placing a strip or two of masking tape on the underside. Alternatively, you can buy clear stick-on pads which will keep templates and rulers from slipping.

4 Using fabric scissors, carefully cut out all the patches along the cutting lines. Set aside the large squares for the moment.

QUILT PLAN

STITCHING

1 Lay out the four small squares that will make up one four-patch block, positioning them as they will appear in the quilt. Pin and stitch both pairs, and then stitch the two sets of pairs together, carefully matching the short seams where they intersect. Repeat this for all seventeen four-patch blocks.

2 On a large flat surface, lay out the large floral squares alternating with the four-patch blocks following the quilt plan. Pin and stitch all the blocks in each horizontal strip. Now stitch the strips together, pinning at the beginning and end of the strip and where the blocks intersect. Stitch the strips together in pairs (1 to 2, 3 to 4, 5 to 6). Then stitch 1-2 to 3-4 and 5-6 to 7. Stitch the final seam.

3 Press the quilt top carefully, first from the back and then the front. Press seams towards the darker fabric or to reduce bulk where the seams meet.

4 Spread the quilt top out, right side up, on a hard flat surface and place the saucer in one corner of the quilt so that it just touches each side (**diagram 1**). Use a fabric marker to draw a curve around the saucer. Repeat for each corner and trim excess fabric away.

DIAGRAM 1

FINISHING

1 Pin the rick rack in place around the edge of the quilt top, placing the centre of the rick rack exactly on the seam lines at the edge. Start and end near, but not at, a corner. Instead of seaming the two ends of the rick rack together, overlap them, curving the loose ends outwards towards the edge of the quilt (**diagram 2**). Stitch the rick rack in place with a backstitch down the centre.

DIAGRAM 2

2 Spray baste the layers to make the quilt sandwich. Trim the backing and wadding to the same size as the quilt top. Now gently pull the edges of the quilt top and the backing fabric away from the wadding, and trim another generous ⅛ in (3 mm) off the wadding. Smooth the fabrics back in place and turn the edges of the quilt top under, rolling it over the edge of the wadding so that the points of the rick rack that were facing the middle are now just visible beyond the outside edge. Fold under the ¼ in (0.75 cm) seam allowance on the backing and slip stitch it in place over the line of backstitches, securing the rick rack (**diagram 3**).

DIAGRAM 3

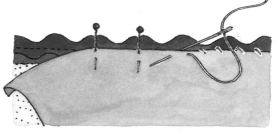

3 Using a quilter's ruler and the Hera marker, mark the diagonal quilting lines as shown on the quilt plan. Using a single strand of the coton à broder and the needle of your choice, quilt along the marked lines taking large ¼ in (0.75 cm) stitches. Normally the quilting would progress from the centre outwards so that any wrinkles can be smoothed out to the edges, however, on this little quilt I would suggest you quilt all the diagonal lines in one direction first, then complete the diagonal lines in the other direction.

Rotary Cutting Techniques

Take your first steps in rotary cutting and machine piecing. Learn how to use the revolutionary rotary cutter and discover speed, accuracy, economy and simplicity in a stroke. Directions for left-handed stitchers are given in brackets.

LEARNING TO USE A ROTARY CUTTER AND RULER

To prepare your fabric for cutting, fold it twice lengthwise with the fold parallel to the selvedges. Press to hold everything together and to reduce shifting of the layers. Place the fabric on your cutting mat with the fold at the top and along one of the grid lines of the mat. If you are right-handed, you will be measuring and making cuts from the left end of the fabric (or from the right end if you are left-handed). You will need to neaten up the raw ends along the crossways grain. Line up a square ruler along the folded edge, and place a 15 x 30 cm (6 x 12-in) ruler to the left of the square ruler, keeping the ruler edges together. Remove the square ruler and cut away a small portion of the left side of the fabric. (If you are left-handed, reverse this process. You now have a clean, straight edge from which to cut strips.

To cut strips, move the 15 x 30 cm (6 x 12-in) ruler to the right, matching the ruler line for the desired width to the freshly cut edges. Cut a strip. Place your left (right) hand flat on the ruler and slightly towards the left (right) side of it so that you are pressing it down and keeping it from slipping sideways at the same time. Holding the cutter so that the blade is standing flat against the edge of the ruler, roll the blade along the edge of the ruler, onto the fabric and off the other side all in one smooth motion. The blade is very sharp so you will need only firm, not hard, pressure on it even though you are cutting through four layers of fabric.

Before cutting any more strips, unfold this one and check that the strip is straight and not V-shaped **(A)**. The grain line must be kept straight throughout the folds of the fabric, and the crosshairs of the ruler must be lined up even with the fold and the grain in order to produce straight strips. If necessary re-fold your fabric and start again.

Cut as many strips as you need, making one cut after the other. You may have to straighten up the angle of the strip again if it starts to become inaccurate.

Once you have cut the necessary numbers of strips, you may need to reduce some of them to shorter strip lengths or squares. Lay one strip on the mat so that it is folded in half only once and the fold is to your right (left). Place one edge of the strip against one of the long lines of the mat and trim off the selvedges. To cut a square, simply align the end of the strip with the appropriate measurement and cut **(B)**.

For rectangles, short strips or any measurement greater than the width of your ruler, turn the ruler and use it lengthways. With practice you will be able to stack the strips and cut several layers at once.

STRIP SETS

Strip sets are used when you wish to quickly produce simple repetitive units from the same fabrics. For instance, in the Stepping Out quilt on page 21, the centres of the blocks are composed of three squares. Instead of cutting and stitching these individually each

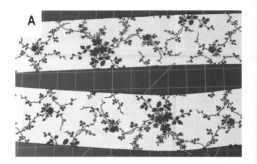

A

time, you can piece three strips into one length which is then cross-cut into segments of the correct size.

Cut the depth of the strips the same size as the finished squares plus seam allowances. Cut the strips across the width of the fabric, remove the selvedges and trim all to the same length. Fold and lightly finger-press the strips to mark the centres and quarter points. Place the middle and one of the side strips right sides together, matching the marks and pinning. Stitch the long seam, taking the usual ¼ in (0.75 cm) seam

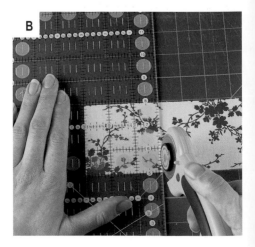

B

allowance. You will need to press each seam before crossing it with another one. Press carefully, usually towards the darker fabric unless instructed otherwise, taking care not to curve or stretch the seams. Place the remaining strip right side down over the middle strip. Match and pin the guide marks, and stitch and press as before.

Place the strip set right side down on the cutting mat aligning it with one of the long lines of the mat. The ends may be slightly uneven so make your first cut wider than you need, turn it and trim to the correct width, which is the width of the finished unit plus seam allowances (**C**). For accuracy when cutting, line up the seams and the edges of the strips with the guidelines of your ruler.

CHAIN PIECING

Chain piecing is another quick and efficient method which you should get into the habit of using whenever possible. Simply put, it means stitching the seams on successive units without breaking the thread in between. It helps to organize the patches into groups next to your sewing machine ready for stitching. When you have sewn the first pair, run the machine on for a few stitches before feeding the next pair under the presser foot. Continue like this until all the pairs are stitched. When you finish you have a line of pieced units strung out like pennants that only have to be clipped apart (**D**). This is a great way to save time and effort – and thread!

TYING A QUILT

If you want to finish a quilt in double-quick time then tying is the answer. In its simplest form the layers are tied together in a grid. Use a sturdy thread such as coton à broder or linen and a slightly larger needle than you

NOTE:

Unlike hand piecing where the seam allowances are left unstitched, when piecing by machine you stitch from cut edge to cut edge.

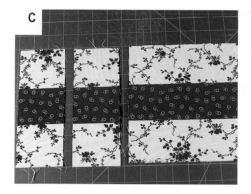

C

would for quilting. You can mark a grid over the quilt or use points on the patchwork. You can tie in the middle of patches (easy) or at seam junctions (slightly less easy since you have to get through several more layers of fabric). You can tie from the front or the back.

There are options to suit every quilt. You may have to experiment to find the best needle for you and the thread you have chosen. Some suggestions are size 7, 5 or 3 betweens quilting needles or a large-eye embroidery needle or, my favourite choice, a Sashiko needle (the kind used for Japanese Sashiko quilting).

Generally I use coton à broder thread for tying, as there is a reasonably large range of

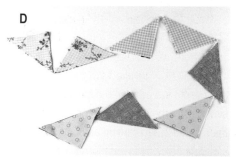

D

colours available. Linen thread is very strong but colour choice is limited to the usual neutrals. Embroidery thread is another possible choice because of the huge palette available, but it needs to be used in multiple strands to be strong enough.

Thread your needle with a long length of thread, approximately 2 yds (2 m) long. Pull the thread through the needle so that it is double but don't knot the ends. Starting from the right side (left if you are left-handed) take a stitch through all three layers at the position

of the first tie. Pull the thread through until there is only about a 4 in (10 cm) tail left. Without stopping to cut the thread, take another stitch at the next position, but leaving a long loose length of thread between the two. Continue in this way across the quilt until you have used up the thread in the needle. Clip the long loose lengths of thread apart, and knot the loose ends (see page 24). Trim the ends to about ¼ in (0.75 cm) (**E**). Adjust the amount of thread you need between the ties to suit yourself. Also you may find it easier to tie in sections rather than rows.

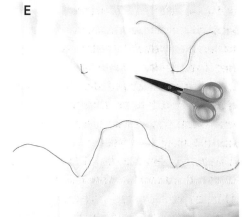

E

BINDING A QUILT

A separate four-piece binding makes a neat and easy finish for the edges. You can use ready-made bias binding, but it is much nicer to use a good quality 100% cotton fabric like the ones in your quilt. There is no need to use a binding cut on the bias unless your quilt has curved edges. For strength I would always use a double straight binding, cutting strips 2½ in (6 cm) deep along the straight grain of the fabric. Cut widthways, unless instructed otherwise. You may need to join strips. In that case join them so that the seam is on the bias. This reduces the bulk when the binding is folded over to the back. To join on the bias, place the left end of one strip over the right end of another, right sides together. They will form a cross. Draw a diagonal line from the upper left to the point on the lower right where they cross **(F)**. Pin and stitch along the line. Trim the seam allowance to ¼ in (0.75 cm). Press the seam open and trim off any "dog-ears" that stick out.

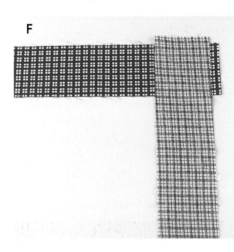

Press the binding strips in half lengthways with wrong sides together **(G)**. Trim two binding strips to the same size as the sides of the quilt; set the other two aside for the moment. Fold and mark the midpoint and quarter points on the two strips and on the sides of the quilt. Position the binding strip against the right-hand edge of the quilt aligning the cut edges of the binding with the edge of the quilt and having the folded edge of the binding pointing towards the middle. Match and pin the centre and quarter points and

G

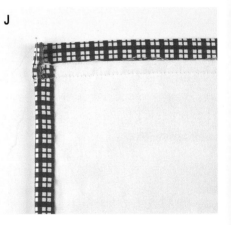

both ends. Using the walking foot attachment on your sewing machine, stitch the binding to the quilt with the usual ¼ in (0.75 cm) seam. Repeat for the binding on the opposite side. Take the folded edge of the binding over to the back of the quilt and slip-stitch in place along the seam line **(H)**.

H

Measure the width of the quilt with the binding in place, and add 1 in (2.5 cm). Cut the remaining two binding strips to that measurement. Measure and mark the centre and quarter points of the binding strips and the edges of the quilt. Pin one binding strip to the top of the quilt, positioning it so that the centre and quarter points match and there are equal amounts extending from each side of the quilt. Stitch the binding to the quilt.

Trim the ends of the binding leaving ¼ in (0.75 cm) sticking out **(I)**. Pull the folded edge of the binding up, but don't take it over to the back just yet.

I

Turn the extra ¼ in (0.75 cm) in neatly at both ends **(J)**.

J

Fold the binding in place on the back and pin. Slipstitch in place along the seam line and stitch the folded ends together neatly **(K)**.

K

"Stepping Out" Quilt

This quilt will give you lots of practice cutting strips and introduce you to some basic time-saving techniques, such as strip sets and chain piecing. Only two fabrics are used in the quilt top, which is tied rather than quilted.

Finished size: 62½ x 62½ in (150 x 150 cm)

MATERIALS

All fabrics used in the quilt top are 45 in (115 cm) wide, 100% cotton

Main fabric: lilac textured pattern, 2⅓ yds (2.1 m)

Second fabric: large floral pattern, 2⅓ yds (2.1 m)

Backing and binding: lilac tonal fabric, 3⅔ yds (3.4 m)

Wadding: lightweight (2 oz) polyester, 68 x 68 in (170 x 170 cm)

Rotary cutter, ruler and cutting mat

Thread: sewing thread to tone with both fabrics, coton à broder no. 16, 4 skeins

Sashiko needle

CUTTING

1 From the main lilac textured fabric, cut the following:

● 22 strips across the width of the fabric, 3 in (7.5 cm) deep.

● From nine of these strips, cross-cut each one into three lengths of 13 in (31.5 cm), avoiding the selvedges. You will need 26 so discard one and set the rest aside.

● From ten of the full-width strips, cross-cut each strip into five lengths of 8 in (19.5 cm), avoiding the selvedges. Set these 50 strips aside.

● Remove the selvedges from the remaining full-width strips and trim each of them to 44 in (112 cm) long.

2 From the second fabric, cut the following:

● 21 strips across the width of the fabric, 3 in (7.5 cm) deep.

● From eight of these strips, cross-cut each one into three lengths of 13 in (31.5 cm), avoiding the selvedges. Set these 24 strips aside.

● From ten of the full-width strips, cross-cut each strip into five lengths of 8 in (19.5 cm), avoiding the selvedges. Set these 50 strips aside.

● Remove the selvedges from the three remaining full-width strips and trim each of them to 44 in (112 cm) long.

3 Cut the backing fabric into two equal lengths of 66 in (170 cm). Remove the selvedges. From each length, cut two strips 2½ in (6 cm) wide down the full length of the fabric to be used for the binding. Set the backing and binding strips aside.

QUILT PLAN

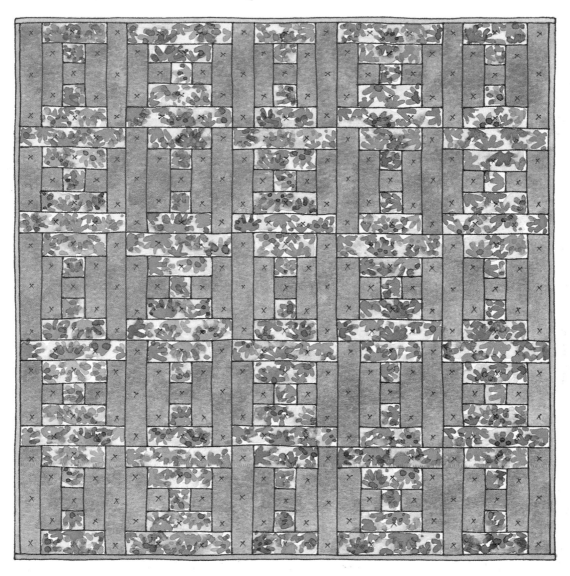

STITCHING

1 There are two different colourways for the block in this quilt. Block A is predominantly lilac and Block B is predominantly floral **(diagram 1)**. The centre rows of both blocks are cut from strip sets **(diagram 2)**. All seams are sewn with a $\frac{1}{4}$ in (0.75 cm) seam allowance throughout.

DIAGRAM 1

Block A   Block B

DIAGRAM 2

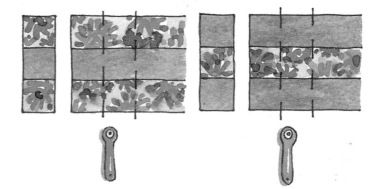

Strip set A   Strip set B

2 Using the diagrams as a guide and the six 44 in (112 cm) long strips, stitch one strip set A (consisting of two floral patterned strips with a lilac textured strip in the middle) and one strip set B (consisting of two lilac textured strips with a floral strip in the middle). In this case, press the seams away from the middle strip. From strip set A cross-cut 13 segments, each 3 in (7.5 cm) wide. From strip set B cross-cut 12 segments, each 3 in (7.5 cm) wide.

3 For the block As, place one strip set A on top of one 8 in (19.5 cm) lilac strip, right sides together. Pin and stitch with the strip set on top so that you can make sure the seam allowances lie in the right direction. Stitch the seam along the right-hand side of the strips. Chain piece all 13 pairs. Clip them apart and press all the seams away from the centre strip sets. Chain piece the 8 in (19.5 cm) lilac strips to the opposite side of the strip set. Cut apart and press seams away from the centre. Stitch the 8 in (19.5 cm) floral strips to the top and bottom of the blocks, pressing seams away from the centre. Finally add the 13 in (31.5 cm) lilac strips to the sides of the blocks, pressing as before **(diagram 3)**.

NOTE:
Use the end of your seam ripper to hold and guide the fabric.

DIAGRAM 3

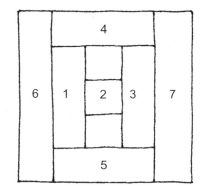

4 The twelve block Bs are stitched in the same manner but reversing the fabric placement. Refer to diagrams 1 and 3 while stitching to help you keep them in the correct order.

5 Following the quilt plan on page 23, lay all the quilt blocks out on a large flat surface, alternating blocks A and B. Stitch all the blocks in each horizontal strip together. Press the seams of each strip in alternating directions. Pin and stitch the long seams together. The alternately pressed seams between the blocks should interlock and help to align them correctly. Press all of the long seams towards the bottom of the quilt.

6 Stitch the two lengths of backing fabric, right sides together, along the 66 in (170 cm) length. Press the seam to one side.

FINISHING

1 Measure the quilt top and cut the backing and wadding at least 2 in (5 cm) bigger on all sides. Spread the backing out on a large flat surface, right side down, with the wadding on top. Spread the quilt over the wadding, right side up. Make sure all three layers are free from wrinkles. Tack the quilt together with enough safety pins to keep the layers from shifting.

2 Using the Sashiko needle and a single strand of the coton à broder doubled over, tie in reef knots across the surface of the quilt **(diagram 4)**. Refer to the quilt plan as a guide for placing the ties.

DIAGRAM 4

3 Remove any pins from the edges of the quilt and trim away excess wadding and backing fabric using your rotary cutter and ruler, squaring up the corners as you cut.

4 Use the four strips cut from the lengths of backing fabric to bind the edges of the quilt with a double straight binding.

Cutting Triangles

It's time to add triangles to your rotary cutting repertoire. The quilt that follows on pages 27–32 uses them not only in the patchwork design but also in the simple setting.

HALF-SQUARE TRIANGLES

Learning to cut half-square triangles is the next logical stage after squares and rectangles. A half-square triangle is formed by dividing a square once, diagonally.

DIAGRAM 1

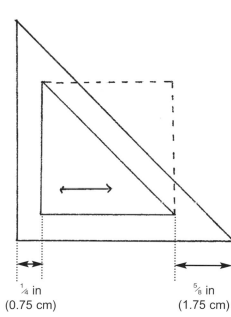

$\frac{1}{4}$ in
(0.75 cm)

$\frac{5}{8}$ in
(1.75 cm)

The right angle of the triangle is cut parallel to the weave of the fabric, and is used where you want the sides of the right angle to be on the straight grain. Because of the extra fabric needed for seam allowances, you should cut squares which are $\frac{7}{8}$ in (2.5 cm) larger than the short side of the triangle you intend to finish up with **(diagram 1)**. To cut half-square triangles, first determine the size of square which you need to cut to give you the correct size of the finished triangle (if this information isn't already provided).

Remember, the square should be cut $\frac{7}{8}$ in (2.5 cm) larger than the short side of the finished triangle. Cut the strips to this depth across the width of the fabric. Cross-cut the strips into squares, avoiding the selvedges. Position your ruler diagonally across one of the squares so that the edge of your ruler falls precisely on the two opposite corner points. Slice the square into two half-square triangles **(A)**.

The piecing of the triangles will vary according to the different patterns you use, as will the pressing. Do take care not to stretch the block out of shape while pressing a diagonal seam.

DESIGNING IS CHILD'S PLAY

So many people feel that they haven't the ability to design their own quilts, but actually all they have to do is play! Most traditional patchwork patterns are composed of simple geometric shapes. Try rearranging those shapes that make up a block. Buy some gridded paper and draw out the block design for the quilt in this chapter. Cut the block into nine squares. Shuffle them around. Or draw several repeats of the original block and make some photocopies. Colour the blocks using only black, white and grey to represent dark, light and medium coloured fabrics. See how many different patterns you can come up with. When you find one you particularly like, interpret it in fabric by placing your dark fabrics where the black shapes are, light fabrics where the white shapes are and so forth. If you also think how many different coloured and patterned fabrics are available, the possibilities become endless.

A

MACHINE QUILTING AS YOU GO

If you like the idea of making a quilt but the idea of quilting it afterwards is stopping you, then this method could be the key. The blocks are pieced and quilted at the same time. To do this you will need to cut a square of backing fabric and one of wadding, both about 1 in (2.5 cm) larger on each side than the finished block. Place a square of the backing fabric, right side down, on a flat surface. Centre the square of wadding over the backing and pin the four corners with safety pins. Mark the middle of each side with straight pins. For our example the completed blocks are positioned "on point" (diagonally) on top of the wadding/backing. Using the midpoints as a guide, position the blocks centrally and secure all three layers with pins, avoiding the seam lines along which the block will be quilted (**B**).

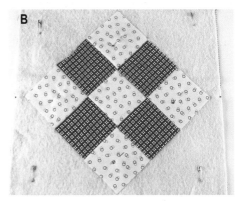

Machine quilt through all three layers with straight lines stitched "in the ditch" e.g. exactly in the seam line along the major seams, using the walking foot attachment on your sewing machine (**C**).

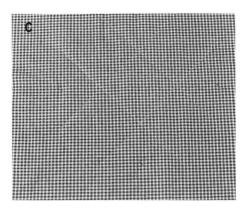

Pull the quilting threads through to the front of the block and tie them off; they will be hidden between the layers. Finally, stitch one of the remaining half-square triangles in place on one side of the centre block, taking a $\frac{1}{4}$ in (0.75 cm) seam allowance through all three layers. Flip the triangle and fingerpress it outwards towards the corner (**D**).

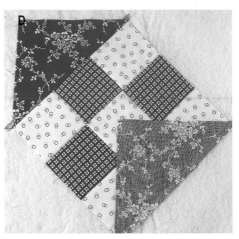

Repeat for the corner opposite and then the two remaining corners (**E**). When you have completed all the quilted blocks, you will need to trim them to the final size plus

seam allowances, squaring them up as you do so. Now you are ready to stitch the quilt together. You need short binding strips to cover the seams between the blocks and long ones for the horizontal seams. You may need to join strips (on the bias) to the required length. Fold all the strips in half, lengthways, and press. Place the first two blocks, right sides together, and matching up

all the block edges. Place a folded binding strip over the seam to be stitched, having the folded edge of the binding pointing towards the middle of the block and matching the cut edges with the edges of the blocks. Pin and stitch the normal $\frac{1}{4}$ in (0.75 cm) seam allowance using the walking foot attachment on your sewing machine (**F**).

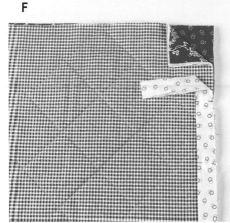

Open out the blocks and trim away as much of the wadding from the seam allowance as you can, being very careful to keep all the fabric out of the way. Fingerpress the folded binding strip over the raw edges of the seam allowance so that it lies flat, and slip stitch in place (**G**).

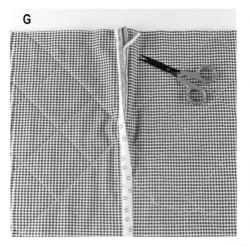

Continue stitching all the short binding strips in place this way, and then do the same for the long strips. Bind the outer edges of the quilt to finish.

"Designing a Rose Garden" Quilt

If at first glance this quilt appears to be made from various blocks rather than repeating the same one, it is only because I have used the fabrics in different places within each block. Each block is quilted separately. When your blocks are finished, so is the quilting.

Finished size: 38 x 51 in (102 x 136 cm)

MATERIALS

All fabrics used in the quilt top are 45 in (115 cm) wide, 100% cotton
Main feature fabric used in centres of blocks and large corner triangles: large rose patterned fabric, 1⅔ yds (1.5 m)
Alternate large corner triangles and binding strips: co-ordinating small floral patterned fabric, 1½ yds (1.4 m)
Block pattern: medium value polka dot, ¾ yd (70 cm)★
Block pattern: light medium plaid, ¾ yd (70 cm)★
Block pattern: plain cream, 1 yd (90 cm)★
Backing squares: two contrasting fabrics, 1½ yds (1.4 m) of each
Wadding: 100% cotton, 45 x 60 in (115 x 152 cm)
Rotary cutter, ruler and cutting mat
Thread: sewing thread to tone with fabrics, invisible machine quilting thread
★These amounts are generous to allow for cutting extra patches to design your own choice of blocks.

CUTTING

1 From the main rose-patterned fabric, cut the following:
● three strips 7¼ in (18.4 cm) deep across the width of the fabric. Cross-cut each strip into four 7¼ in (18.4 cm) squares, avoiding the selvedges. Divide each square in half diagonally once, giving 24 half-square triangles. Set aside.
● two strips 3½ in (9 cm) deep across the width of the fabric. Cross-cut into twelve 3½ in (9 cm) squares, avoiding the selvedges, for the centres of the blocks.
● six strips 2½ in (6 cm) deep across the width of the fabric. Set these aside for binding the edges of the quilt.

2 From the co-ordinating small floral patterned fabric, cut the following:
● three strips 7¼ in (18.4 cm) deep across the width of the fabric. Cross-cut each strip into four 7¼ in (18.4 cm) squares, avoiding the selvedges. Divide each square in half diagonally once, giving 24 half-square triangles. Set aside.
● seven strips 2 in (5 cm) deep across the width of the fabric. From each of four of these, cut two strips 15 in (38 cm) long. Set these eight short and three long strips aside for covering the seams on the back.

3 From the polka dot fabric, cut the following:
● two strips 3⅞ in (10 cm) deep across the width of the fabric. Cross-cut each strip into six 3⅞ in (10 cm) squares, avoiding the selvedges. Slice each square diagonally once to give a total of 24 half-square triangles.
● four strips 2 in (5.25 cm) deep across the width of the fabric. From each strip, cut ten segments 3½ in (9 cm) long, avoiding the

QUILT PLAN

selvedges. This will give you a few extra to play with.

4 From the plaid fabric, cut the following:

• two strips 3⅞ in (10 cm) deep across the width of the fabric. Cross-cut each strip into eight 3⅞ in (10 cm) squares, avoiding the selvedges. Slice each square diagonally once giving a total of 32 half-square triangles.

• one strip 3½ in (9 cm) deep across the width of the fabric. Cross-cut the strip into four 3½ in (9 cm) squares, avoiding the selvedges.

• two strips 2 in (5.25 cm) deep across the width of the fabric. Cross-cut each strip into ten segments 3½ in (9 cm) long.

5 From the plain cream fabric, cut the following:

• three strips 3⅞ in (10 cm) deep across the width of the fabric. From each strip cut seven 3⅞ in (10 cm) squares, avoiding the selvedges. Divide the squares diagonally once to give 42 half-square triangles.

• five strips 2 in (5.25 cm) deep across the width of the fabric. From each strip cut ten segments 3½ in (9 cm) wide, avoiding the selvedges.

6 From one of the backing fabrics, cut the following:

• three strips 15 in (38 cm) deep across the width of the fabric. Cross-cut each strip into two 15 in (38 cm) squares, avoiding the selvedges.

• Repeat for the other backing fabric. Set all 12 squares aside.

7 From the wadding, cut the following:

• 12 squares 15 x 15 in (38 x 38 cm). Set aside.

STITCHING

1 Study the quilt plan on page 29 and the traditional American block, known as Churn Dash (**diagram 2**). Also take some time to familiarize yourself with the small diagrams of the separate units of the block showing the different fabric combinations and the numbers needed of each (**diagram 1**). After stitching all these units, be sure to take some time to arrange and re-arrange them to see how many different block designs you can find. Let the creative child within you loose again. If you prefer your ideas to mine, then congratulations, you've just designed your first quilt!

DIAGRAM 1

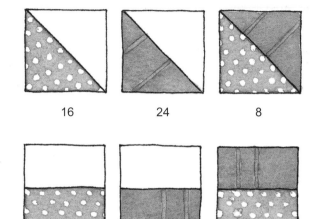

16   24   8

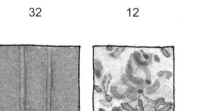

32   12   4

2   10

DIAGRAM 2

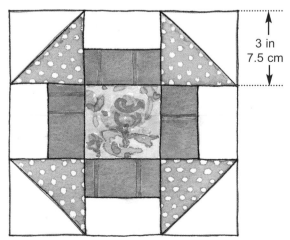

3 in
7.5 cm

2 Start with the triangle units. Put the triangles near your machine with each fabric in a stack. Pick up the first pair, for instance, a plain cream and a polka dot, and place them right sides together with all sides matching. Taking the usual ¼ in (0.75 cm) seam allowance throughout, stitch them together along the long side of the triangle. As both of these edges are cut on the bias, take care not to stretch them while stitching or pressing. Chain piece the numbers of different pairs indicated in diagram 1. Do the same for the three pairs of rectangles, placing them right sides together, matching all cut edges and stitching them together along the long side of the rectangle. Snip all the pairs apart and press each unit towards the darker fabric.

3 When you have decided on the layout of all 12 blocks, you are ready to stitch them together. Lay out the units for the first block as they will appear in the finished block. Beginning with the top row of units, flip the middle unit over, right sides together, on top of the left-hand one, matching all the cut edges. Pin and stitch them together along the right-hand side. Do not cut the thread but place the same two units from the next strip, right sides together and edges aligned, under the presser foot and continue stitching along the right-hand side. Repeat for the same two units in the last strip. Now break the thread and remove the chain. Leave them held together by the little thread "bridges" while you finish the block. Open out the first two pairs and place the third unit from that strip

right side down on top of the middle one, matching the three raw edges. Stitch together along the right side and continue adding to the second and third strips in this way. Break the thread and remove the partially finished block held together in strips. Press the seams of the top and bottom strips towards the middle unit. Press the seams of the centre strip towards the outer units. Flip the top strip over the middle one. Pin and stitch. Repeat for the last strip. Press the long seams down. Complete the remaining 11 blocks in the same way.

FINISHING

1 Lay your completed blocks out on a large flat surface and move them around until you are happy with the arrangement. Pin an identifying number to each block, and pin the block to a square of wadding and the appropriate backing fabric so as to form a chequerboard pattern on the back of the finished quilt. Organizing your work at this stage will save you much time and effort later.

2 Starting with the first block, layer the backing square and wadding and secure with pins. Mark the midpoints of all four sides. Position the block centrally on the wadding matching the corners of the block with the pins marking the midpoints. Secure the block with safety pins. Using your sewing machine and walking foot attachment, quilt in the ditch down the four middle seam lines to form an "X", starting and stopping at the block edges **(diagram 3)**. Pull the threads through to the front; tie and trim the ends.

3 Add the setting triangles. Starting with the rose patterned fabric, pinch-mark the midpoint of the long edge of the triangle. Place it right side down on the upper left side of the quilted block, matching midpoint to midpoint and aligning the edges of both. Pin and stitch the seam through all three layers, taking the usual ¼ in (0.75 cm) seam allowance. Flip and fingerpress the quilted seam. Reposition the safety pin to hold all three layers together

DIAGRAM 3

until the block is completed. Stitch the second rose-patterned triangle to the opposite side of the block in the same way. Then add the other patterned triangles to the remaining two sides. Finally, don't forget to pin the identifying number back in place. Complete each block in this manner.

4 Stitch the blocks together using the short 2 in (5 cm) wide strips. Slip stitch the binding in place to cover the raw edges of the seam allowances. Using the three long 2 in (5 cm) wide binding strips, stitch the long strips together and slip stitch the binding in place to cover the raw edges.

5 Use the 2½ in (6 cm) wide binding strips to bind the edges of the quilt with a double straight binding.

Further Triangle Techniques

Learn how to identify and use the other most frequently encountered triangle, the quarter-square triangle. This section also shows you how to create mitred borders for your quilts.

QUARTER-SQUARE TRIANGLES

Quarter-square triangles are made by dividing a square twice, diagonally. They are cut with the long side of the triangle on the straight grain of the fabric and both sides of the right angle on the bias (diagram 1).

DIAGRAM 1

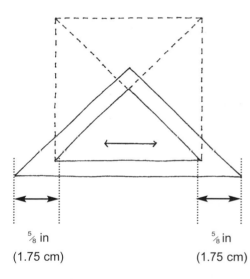

5/8 in
(1.75 cm)

5/8 in
(1.75 cm)

A

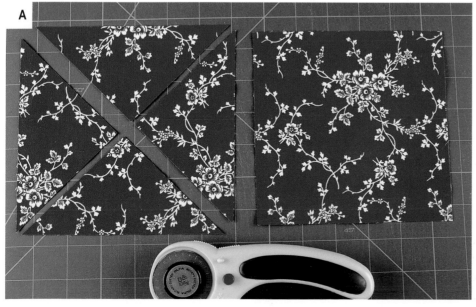

NOTE:

I use another small, self-healing mat which I find very useful for cutting quarter-square triangles. Simply turn the mat to make the second cut. When calculating how many squares you will need, remember that you will get four triangles for every square. Piecing instructions for these triangles will vary with different blocks, but always take care when stitching and pressing the (bias-cut) sides of the right angle.

Like the half-square triangle, you start with a large square; in this case the size of the square is $1\frac{1}{4}$ in (3.5 cm) larger than the finished size of the long side of the triangle. This greater length takes into account the extra seam allowances. Again, like the half-square triangle, you start by cutting a strip to the required depth across the width of your fabric. Cross-cut this into squares which are then cut diagonally, twice (A). Make the first diagonal cut, then without moving the cut square, make the second diagonal cut in the opposite direction.

SETTING (PLACING) QUILT BLOCKS ON THE DIAGONAL

Diagonal settings have a more dynamic and energetic feeling to them. They also have the ability to make very simple blocks look more complicated than they actually are.

The blocks are still stitched together in long strips, but the length of the strips will vary and require quarter- and/or half-square triangles at both ends to finish them off. The end triangles are turned in different directions. And you may have a half- or a quarter-square triangle at both ends, or different ones at each end, depending on the size and shape of the quilt. When stitching a quarter-square triangle to a block, match the right angle of the triangle to the corner of the block; the long point of the triangle will extend beyond the edge of the block at the other end of the seam. When stitching half-square triangles to blocks, you will need to find and mark the mid-point of the long side and match it to the mid-point of the block; the long points of the triangle will extend beyond the edges of the block.

In order to keep the quilt from stretching out of shape, it is preferable to have all the outside edges of the triangles on the straight grain. Therefore, use half-square triangles at the corners because they have their right angles on the straight grain, and use quarter-square triangles around the sides because they have their long side on the straight grain. The position of the grain lines determines which type of triangle to use.

MITRED BORDERS

Mitred borders look especially nice on diagonally-set quilts. They do require a bit of care but are definitely worth the effort. The quilt on pages 36–40 has two borders making a total of eight mitred corners. Never fear! The simple shortcut is to stitch the two border strips together and treat as one, reducing the number of mitres to four.

Fold and pinch-mark the midpoint of the border strips. Place one of these strips along the right edge of the quilt, right sides together, matching the midpoints. Measure from the midpoint to the corner on the quilt. Measure off the same amount on the border strip and pin. Fold to find the quarter point between these two marks and pin again. Repeat on the other side of the midpoint.

Stitch the border to the quilt, starting and ending exactly at the corners with a back-stitch. Do not stitch into the seam allowance at the corners.

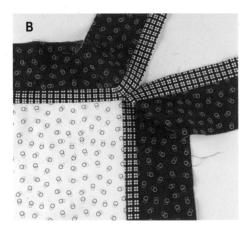

NOTE:
Try not to lose any sleep over points that aren't perfect. Just do the best you can, and if you don't get it right each time, remember that little imperfections are what gives a quilt its character.

Stitch the other three borders to the quilt in exactly the same way. All four border strips will just touch at the corners, but all the ends of these strips will be left loose (**B**). Press the seams towards the borders.

Place the quilt on a large, flat surface, right side up. Starting in the upper right-hand corner of the quilt, smooth the right-hand border straight up. Smooth the top border over it forming a cross (**C**).

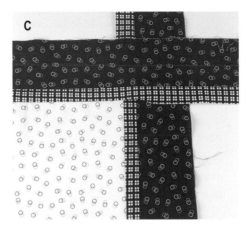

Take the corner of the top border under and up to form a 45-degree mitred fold. The folded end which sticks out should line up exactly with the extended end of the right border, and the seam line between the narrow and wide borders should match (**D**).

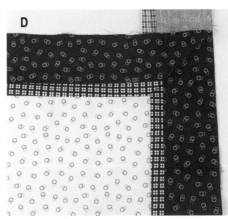

Pin and press the fold line, but do not trim away the excess fabric just yet. Give the quilt a quarter turn, and follow the same procedure for the lower right-hand corner and so on, until you have pinned and pressed the folds on all four corners.

Starting with the upper right corner again, place pins in the excess fabric at the back of the mitre to keep it from shifting. When you have done this, remove the pins from the front. Fold the whole quilt diagonally, right sides together, with the border strips extending out from the corner (**E**). Making sure the seam lines and the edges of the border strips are aligned, pin to secure.

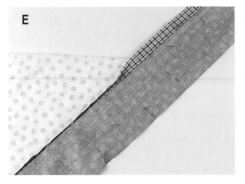

Keeping the corner of the centre seam allowance out of the way, stitch the mitre using the pressed fold as your guideline. Stitch from the inner to the outer corner, beginning and ending with a few backstitches (**F**). Be careful not to stretch the fabrics.

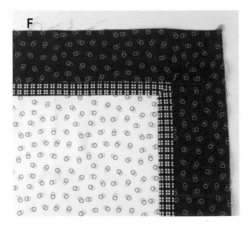

Stitch the other three corners in the same way, re-folding the quilt each time and making sure you align the seams and the edges of the borders.

Alternatively, you can carefully slip stitch the folded mitre in place by hand from the front once you have pinned it. Matching seam lines or stripes in the fabric is easier with this method because you can see both sides of the mitre at the same time.

Trim away the seam allowances to $\frac{1}{4}$ in (0.75 cm). You can press the seams open if they have been stitched by machine, but I would press them to one side if they are hand stitched.

CONTINUOUS BINDING WITH MITRED CORNERS

Cut binding strips across the width of your fabric, $2\frac{1}{2}$ in (6 cm) deep. You will need to stitch together enough of these to form a continuous strip at least 10–12 in (25–30 cm) greater than the measurement around the edges of your quilt. Always join the strips along the bias to distribute the extra bulk of the seam when the strips are turned. Trim the beginning and end of this long strip to 45 degrees, cutting in the same direction as the seam lines. On the right-hand end of this long strip, press under a $\frac{1}{4}$ in (0.75 cm) turning. Fold the strip in half down its length, wrong sides together, and press.

With the quilt right side up, place the binding on the right-hand edge, starting about 10 in (25 cm) up from the lower right corner. Have the cut edges of the binding even with the edge of the quilt and the folded edge towards the middle. Pin the binding in place with the last pin marking the corner point. Leaving the first 4–5 in (10–12 cm) of the binding loose, stitch the binding to the quilt using the walking foot attachment on your sewing machine (G). Stitch the seam only as far as the corner point; do not stitch past the corner and do not stitch into the seam allowance. Take a few backstitches and cut the threads.

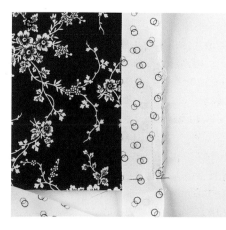

Move the quilt to a flat surface. With the binding you have just stitched positioned on the side away from you, fold the long length of binding up so the fold forms a 45-degree mitre at the corner and the cut edges of the binding extend up, even with the edges of the quilt (H).

Fold the binding back down towards you with the folded edge even with the top edge of the quilt and the cut edges of the binding lining up with the side edge of the quilt. Pin the binding in place along this second side with the last pin marking the corner point as before. Continue stitching the binding to the quilt, starting from the folded edge and stopping exactly at the corner with a few backstitches (I).

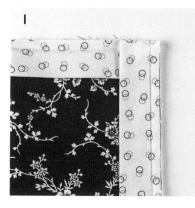

Continue on like this until you are about 10 in (25 cm) from the leading end of the binding strip. Backstitch and cut the threads. Slip the tail end of the binding strip inside the leading section and mark the position of the inner folded edge of the leading section onto the tail end. Cut the tail end of the

binding $\frac{1}{2}$ in (1.5 cm) longer than the marked point (J).

Refold, and slip this end back inside the first. Pin securely and finish stitching the binding in place (K).

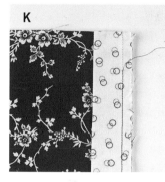

Slipstitch the tucked ends together invisibly along the diagonal seam. Take the folded edge of the binding from the front over to the back, forming mitres at the corners on both the front and back. You will reduce the bulk if you direct the excess fabric inside the mitres in opposite directions on the front and back. Pin the binding in place over the seam line on the back and slip stitch in place (L).

"Water Baby" Quilt

This delightful quilt will provide you with plenty of practice cutting and piecing quarter-square triangles, as well as demonstrating their partnership with half-square triangles when setting quilt blocks on point. The design of this quilt lends itself perfectly to borders and binding with neatly mitred corners.

Finished size: 33½ x 42 in (80 x 100 cm)

MATERIALS

All fabrics used in the quilt top are 45 in (115 cm) wide, 100% cotton
Pinwheels in pieced blocks: bright dotted fabric, ¾ yd (70 cm)
Block backgrounds, alternate plain blocks and setting triangles: bright yellow textured fabric, 1½ yds (1.4 m)
Narrow inner border and binding: striped fabric, ¾ yd (70 cm)
Wide outer border: bright seaside theme fabric, ½ yd (50 cm)
Backing fabric: 1⅓ yds (1.2 m)
Wadding: 100% cotton, 36 x 46 in (90 x 110 cm)
Rotary cutter, ruler and cutting mat
Thread: sewing thread to tone with your fabrics, machine quilting thread to match dotted and yellow textured fabrics
Fabric spray adhesive
Hera marker

CUTTING

1 From the dotted fabric, cut the following:
● two strips each 4¾ in (11.5 cm) deep, across the width of the fabric. Cross-cut these into twelve 4¾ in (11.5 cm) squares, avoiding the selvedges. Set these aside.
● two more strips each 4¼ in (10.6 cm) deep, across the width of the fabric. Cross-cut these into twelve 4¼ in (10.6 cm) squares, avoiding the selvedges. Slice each square diagonally both ways giving you 48 quarter-square triangles. Set these aside.

2 From the yellow textured fabric, cut the following:
● two strips each 6½ in (15.6 cm) deep, across the width of the fabric. Cross-cut these into six 6½ in (15.6 cm) squares, avoiding the selvedges. Set these aside for the alternate plain blocks.
● one strip, 9¾ in (23.5 cm) deep, across the width of the fabric. Cross-cut into three 9¾ in (23.5 cm) squares, avoiding the selvedges. Slice each square diagonally both ways. This will give you twelve quarter-square triangles. Discard two of them and set the other ten aside to be used as setting triangles for the sides of the quilt.
● one strip 5⅛ in (12.5 cm) deep, across the width of the fabric. Cross-cut into two 5⅛ in (12.5 cm) squares, avoiding the selvedges. Slice each square in half diagonally to give you four half-square triangles. Set aside to be used as the setting triangles for the corners.
● two strips across the width of the fabric, each 4¼ in (10.6 cm) deep. Cross-cut these into twelve 4¼ in (10.6 cm) squares, avoiding the selvedges. Slice each square diagonally both ways to give you 48 quarter-square triangles for the block backgrounds. Set aside.

3 From the striped fabric, cut the following:
● four strips each 1½ in (4 cm) deep, across the width of the fabric for the narrow inner

QUILT PLAN

border. Leave the selvedge on these strips for now and set aside.

● four strips from the width of the fabric, each 2½ in (6 cm) deep. Remove the selvedges and set aside for the binding.

4 From the seaside theme fabric, cut the following:

● four strips each 3½ in (9 cm) deep across the width of the fabric for the wide outer border. Do not remove the selvedges. Set aside.

5 Trim the selvedges from the backing fabric. Set aside.

STITCHING

1 Stack all the small quarter-square triangles near your sewing machine. Place the dotted ones to the left and the yellow ones to the right. Flip one yellow triangle over on top of a dotted one, right sides together, and stitch from the point of the triangles towards the right angles **(diagram 1)**. Chain piece all of the sets together in this manner. Snip them apart and press each seam towards the dotted fabric.

2 The pinwheel block has one set of triangles stitched to each side of a dotted square. To position the triangles correctly you will need to mark the midpoint on each side of the

DIAGRAM 1

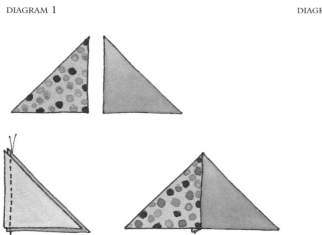

DIAGRAM 3

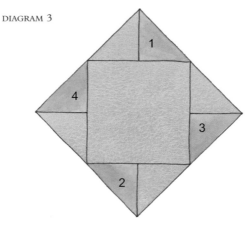

square by folding in half and pinching a crease line. Place a triangle unit on top of the square, right sides together, matching the midpoint with the seam line between the two triangles. Pin and stitch. Chain piece this seam on all of the blocks. Clip apart and chain piece the opposite set of triangles in the same way **(diagrams 2 and 3)**. Clip and press both seams towards the centre square. Stitch the remaining two sides, but this time press the seams towards the triangle units.

them off properly. The triangles are turned in different directions and there may be a different type at each end. Study **diagram 4** carefully and lay out the blocks and triangles in the correct order on a large flat surface. Remember, the four half-square triangles go in the corners and the quarter-square triangles go on the sides of the quilt. Pick up all

DIAGRAM 2

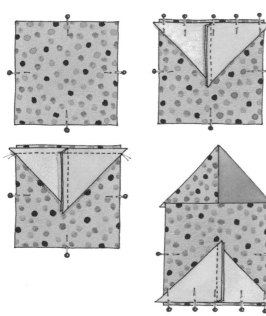

3 The quilt is set on the diagonal, but is still constructed in strips with pieced and plain blocks alternating. The strips require half- or quarter-square triangles at the ends to finish

DIAGRAM 4

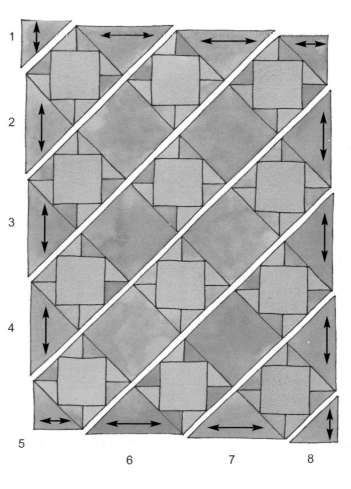

the units that compose a diagonal strip and lay them out in order near your machine so you can reach them easily. Stitch the seams individually, and lay them back in place, checking for accuracy as you go. When the strips are all complete, press the seams away from the pieced blocks. Finally, stitch the strips together, pinning the intersecting seams and at the beginning and end of the strip, and pinch-mark the yellow square blocks and corner triangles to align with the centres of the pieced blocks. Press all the long seams in the same direction.

4 Stitch the narrow striped border strips to the wide border strips. Stitch these four pieced borders to the quilt, mitring the corners. Have the border strip on the bottom while stitching. Stitch just a thread to the right of the block intersections rather than going straight across them. This ensures that the points will be visible when the seam is pressed open.

FINISHING

1 Using fabric spray adhesive, spray baste the layers to form the quilt sandwich. Using the quilt plan as a guide, mark the quilting lines on the quilt.

2 To machine quilt a large item successfully, you need to have the weight of the quilt supported so that it doesn't drag, either forwards or backwards.

Begin stitching in the middle of the quilt and work outwards. Start and end the quilting lines with a few stationary stitches to lock the thread in place. The ends are simply clipped off even with the quilt surface. However, this can result in a noticeable build-up of stitches, especially on the back, so some quilters prefer to leave lengths of thread at the start and finish of the quilting line which are pulled to the back of the quilt for tying and weaving into the wadding.

Quilt over the centre of the quilt, matching the thread to the colour of the blocks being stitched and a bobbin thread to match

NOTE:
When marking quilting lines, you may discover that your blocks don't line up perfectly. Mark the line as straight as possible for as long as you can, then re-position the ruler to one side or the other as necessary. When quilting, simply take one or two stitches sideways in the seam line, and then start off straight again. This method is much less noticeable than missing the corners with the line of quilting. You do not need to mark in-the-ditch quilting lines.

the colour of your backing fabric. Quilt in the ditch around both sides of the narrow striped border. Using a long stitch length, stitch around the outside edges of the quilt, just inside the seam allowance. With your rotary cutter and ruler, trim the outer seam allowance down to ¼ in (0.75 cm), squaring up the corners of the quilt at the same time.

3 Join the four binding strips into one continuous strip and use to bind the quilt, mitring the corners as you go.

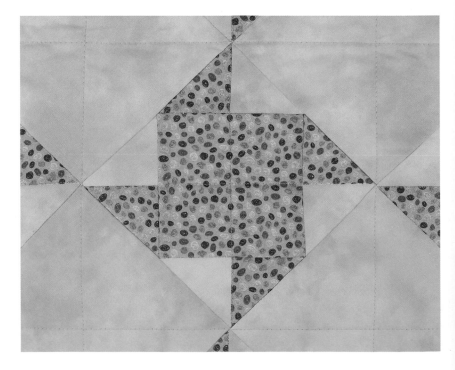

Tricks with Triangles

Now we get to the things your mother never told you. Here's a technique that gives you triangles without tears. You waste a bit of fabric, but it's quick and very accurate.

EASY TRIANGLES FROM SQUARES

This technique allows you to cut and piece half-square triangles quickly and simply. It facilitates accurate pressing as well. A square, cut to the correct size, is first stitched to the corner of the background fabric with a diagonal seam. The triangle that is formed by the stitching is then flipped and pressed, and finally, the excess layers underneath are trimmed away.

To determine the size of the square to cut, add $\frac{1}{2}$ in (1.5 cm) to the finished size of the short side of the triangle. Cut the correct number of squares for your project and mark the back of each with a single diagonal line running from corner to corner. Place a square, right side down, on the correct corner of the background patch, matching the outside corners of both background and square (A). Pin and stitch along the drawn line (B). Flip the resultant half-square triangle over and press in place, using the right angle of the background patch to square up the outer corner of the triangle (C). Flip the triangle back out of the way, and trim the seam allowance to $\frac{1}{4}$ in (0.75 cm) (D). Repeat for each triangle in your project.

ORGANIZING WORK IN PROGRESS

We all lead such busy lives that it is often difficult to set aside much more than snatched moments for our creative activities. Perhaps you are trying to select fabrics to combine in a scrap quilt, but need time to consider your choices before finalizing them. Most of us are not lucky enough to have a dedicated workspace where we can leave projects lying around until they are completed. You might find, however, that such a simple device as a large square of gridded interfacing on which to pin your fabrics would help to keep everything organized between sessions. In the project which follows, I have suggested you try this method for trying out the fabric combinations and for eliminating mistakes while stitching the blocks.

SASHES AND BORDERS

Until now we have set the quilt blocks edge to edge, but there is another option – sashing strips. These strips, which can be either plain or pieced, frame and separate the patterns of the blocks. They can be a calming influence if the blocks are busy or jazz up dull ones. Utilize them to help disguise unequal sized blocks or to add width and length to a quilt. Or simply use them to divide the quilt horizontally and/or vertically (see Join The Flock, page 66).

When deciding on fabric for sashings, choose one that contrasts in some way with the backgrounds of the blocks or else the patchwork pattern will appear to float. Of course, you may decide you prefer that effect. There are no unbreakable rules.

In general, sashing strips are divided into the short ones between the blocks and the longer ones that divide the strips of blocks. Stitching the sashing is very straightforward and logical. The short strips are stitched to the completed blocks; the long ones to the completed strips of blocks.

You may also find the same strips used as an outer frame around all the blocks, although, confusingly, you may also find that referred to as the first border. Borders, like sashing strips, may be elaborate or simple. Indeed, some quilts could be composed almost entirely of borders (see Country Squire's Medallion, page 54).

If you need to size a design to your specific requirements, adding (or subtracting) inches/centimetres to the border is much the simplest way. Another tip to remember, if you see a fabric you simply must own but don't have a specific project in mind for it, buy at least $2\frac{3}{4}$–3 yds (2.5–3 m); that way you will have enough yardage to cut four wide borders running lengthways down the fabric and have enough left over to use in the blocks.

HAND QUILTING

Many people, even those who use quick cutting and piecing techniques, choose to hand quilt, finding it both soothing and therapeutic. The quilt project that follows is just the right size as an introduction to the technique of fine hand quilting – big enough to give you a reasonable taste of what is involved but not so large as to be overwhelming. You will need a betweens needle (I suggest a pack of mixed sizes so you can experiment to find the size that suits you), a glazed quilting thread and two thimbles, one for each hand. Many quilters use a quilting hoop but this is a matter of preference – a hoop that is 14 in (35 cm) in diameter is a good size.

For hand quilting I prefer to tack the quilt layers together with thread, taking long stitches over the whole quilt, in lines about 4–6 in (10–15 cm) apart. Fold the surplus backing over to the front, and stitch it around the edges to keep the wadding from fraying while you are quilting.

Use a Hera marker to draw the quilting lines on the quilt top. Other options are fabric or washable markers, but do take care to test markers on all your fabrics and follow directions for usage. For complicated quilting patterns I prefer to mark the top before tacking the layers together.

If you are using a quilting hoop, spread out your work on a large flat surface and centre the quilt over the inner ring of the hoop. The most common mistake novice quilters make is to stretch the quilt drum tight in the hoop, making it virtually impossible to take a stitch. The needle is rocked up and down guided by the thimble on your dominant hand, and the quilt needs to be slightly "floppy" in order to bring the needle back up through the quilt layers. Place the outer ring over the inner one, but before you tighten the wing nut, press the palm of your hand down in the middle of the hoop to create some slack. Tighten the hoop, check to make sure there are no wrinkles in the front or back and you are ready to go.

Using a single length of quilting thread about 18 in (45 cm) long with a knot in the end you've just cut, insert the needle into the top and wadding only and bring it out at your starting point. Tug on the thread to lodge the knot in the wadding. To make the first stitch, insert the needle straight down through all three layers, then place your thimble on the eye end of the needle ready to continue. The leading edge of the under thimble pushes upwards on the layers making a ridge in the quilt just forward of your needle, and the thumb on your upper hand moves to hold the quilt down on the other side of the ridge. As the needle emerges from the front, it touches the raised edge of the under thimble and is deflected back upwards to form the stitch on the back. Imagine the needle as being an extension of the upper thimble so that the two move as one. Rock the needle back downwards to make the next stitch, moving your under thimble and thumb along also (**E**). Try to take two or three stitches at a time before pulling the thread through, but don't worry if you can't. You will find your own style and rhythm with practice. It also depends on how thick the wadding is, how many layers of fabric you are stitching through and other variables. To fasten off, take the last stitch straight through to the back of the quilt and put a knot in the thread about $\frac{1}{4}$ in (0.75 cm) from the quilt surface. With a backstitch tug the knot into the wadding and clip the tail of thread even with the quilt surface.

E

"Twinkling Stars" Quilt

Make this soft throw or bed quilt using triangles from squares and see for yourself how easy it is. You can also pick up some tips on organizing your work-in-progress to ensure a successful result. Surround the completed blocks with narrow sashing strips and a simple wide border.

Finished size: 64 x 64 in (168 x 168 cm)

MATERIALS

All fabrics used in the quilt top are 45 in (115 cm) wide, 100% cotton
Stars: various plaids, scraps to total 1⅓ yds (1.2 m) (For one star you will need at least 5 x 7 in/12.5 x 18 cm)
Block backgrounds: natural calico, 2½ yds (2.25 m)
Narrow sashings: striped fabric, ⅔ yd (60 cm)
Wide outer border: co-ordinating plaid, 2 yds (1.9 m)
Binding and backing: 3⅞ yds (3.6 m)
Wadding: lightweight (2 oz) polyester, 68 x 68 in (180 x 180 cm)
Rotary cutter, ruler and cutting mat
Gridded interfacing: for each of the nine blocks you will need a square at least 18 x 18 in (50 x 50 cm)
Markers: fabric marking pencil, Hera marker
Threads: sewing thread, quilting thread to match calico

CUTTING

1 From the plaid fabric, cut the following:
● strips 1½ in (4 cm) deep, avoiding any selvedges. Cross-cut these into 1½ in (4 cm) squares. For each of the 36 stars you will need six 1½ in (4 cm) squares, making a total of 216. How many different squares in each fabric you have is up to you. On the wrong side of these squares use your ruler and marking pencil to draw a diagonal line from corner to corner. Set these aside.

2 From the calico, cut the following:
● 23 strips each 3½ in (9.5 cm) deep across the width of the fabric. Cross-cut each strip into ten 3½ in (9.5 cm) squares, avoiding the selvedges, giving a total of 230 squares. Discard five and set the remaining 225 squares aside.

3 From the striped fabric, cut the following:
● ten strips across the width of the fabric 1¼ in (3.5 cm) deep. Trim the selvedges from all the strips and set aside.

4 From the co-ordinating plaid for the outer border, cut the following:
● four strips 8½ in (21.5 cm) wide down the length of the fabric, parallel to but not including the selvedges. To do this, fold the fabric in half with the fold running from selvedge to selvedge, then fold in half again the same way, keeping the selvedges even. If you do not have a second ruler to make up the extra width needed to cut these wide strips, use the markings on your cutting mat, or buy another ruler. Reduce two of the border strips to 48½ in (129.5 cm) in length and the remaining two to 64½ in (169.5 cm).

QUILT PLAN

5 Cut the backing fabric into two lengths of 68 in (180 cm) each. Trim the selvedges off. From each length cut two strips 2½ in (6 cm) wide down the full length of the fabric to be used for the binding. Set aside.

STITCHING

1 Before you start stitching you will need to decide which star fabrics to combine in each block. Using the gridded interfacing, pin the squares together in possible combinations of nine blocks of four stars each. Each of the nine blocks are made up of 25 block units as follows: 4 units have two different star fabrics (A), 4 units have two of the same star fabric triangles (B), 8 units have one star fabric triangle (C) and the remaining 9 units are unpieced squares (**diagram 1**).

DIAGRAM 1

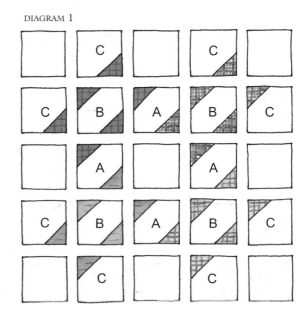

2 Decisions made, remove the squares from the interfacing but pin the units together with safety pins until they are required. Work on one quilt block at a time. Pin 25 calico squares to the interfacing, setting them five squares across by five squares down. Fold the small star squares into triangle shapes and, using the diagram as a guide, pin them to the background squares in the appropriate places **(diagram 2)**. Make sure they are all pointing in the right directions.

DIAGRAM 2

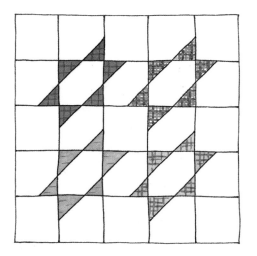

3 Working on one background square at a time, remove it with the star fabric(s) and stitch the triangle(s) in place individually. Notice that some background squares have only one star triangle and some have two. Of those with two, some have two of the same fabric and some have two different fabrics. I found it easiest to stitch the four squares with two different star fabrics first, then the four which had matching star fabrics. Finally, I chain pieced the eight squares which had only one star triangle each.

4 Return each unit to its proper place on the interfacing after it is stitched. Stitch the calico squares into five strips of five squares each. Press the seams of strips one, three and five to the right, and two and four to the left. Stitch the strips together to form the completed block. Press the long seams open to reduce the bulk. Complete all nine blocks in this way.

5 Take two sashing strips, place them right sides together and stitch across the narrow width of the strip. If you are using a striped fabric, carefully match and pin so that the seam line falls along the edge of the stripe and is hidden. Repeat three more times. Press the seams open.

Lay one of the strips out flat. Using a measuring tape, measure off 24½ in (64.75 cm) to the left and to the right of the seam line. Mark and cut the sashing at those points, giving you a pieced sashing 48½ in (129.5 cm) long. Repeat three more times.

From the remnants left over after cutting these, you can cut eight shorter strips, each 15½ in (41.5 cm) long. Cross-cut two more shorter pieces 15½ in (41.5 cm) long from each of the remaining two long lengths. You should now have 12 short and four long sashing strips.

6 Lay your nine completed blocks out in an arrangement that you are happy with. Place the three top blocks near your sewing machine. Stitch a short sash to the right-hand side of each block, right sides together **(diagram 3)**. Stitch the fourth sash to the left-hand side of the first block.

DIAGRAM 3

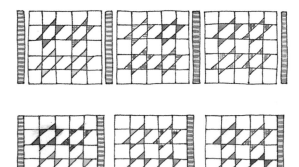

Flip the second block over the first, right sides together, and stitch the seam between the sash and the second block. Add the third block in the same way. Complete the remaining two strips in the same fashion. Press all seams towards the sashing.

Pin and stitch a long pieced sashing strip to both edges of the top strip. Pin and stitch the remaining two long pieced sashing strips to the lower edges of the middle and bottom strips. Pin and stitch both top and bottom strips to the middle one. Press the seams towards the sashing (**diagram 4**).

DIAGRAM 4

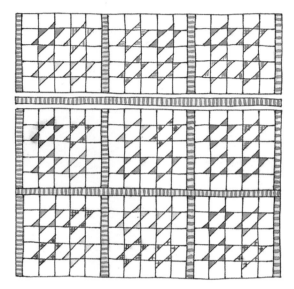

7 Fold and mark the midpoint and the quarter points of the short side border strips and the sides of the quilt. Matching the markings, pin and stitch the right-hand border to the quilt. Repeat for the left-hand border. Press seams towards the sashing. Repeat this process for the top and bottom borders.

FINISHING

1 Place the two lengths of backing fabric right sides together and stitch the long lengthways seam. Press the seam to one side (**diagram 5**).

2 Lay the backing, right side down, on a large flat surface with the wadding on top. Centre the quilt, right side up, over the backing and wadding. Carefully smooth all three layers making sure there are no wrinkles. Using a long needle and a light coloured thread, tack the quilt layers together.

DIAGRAM 5

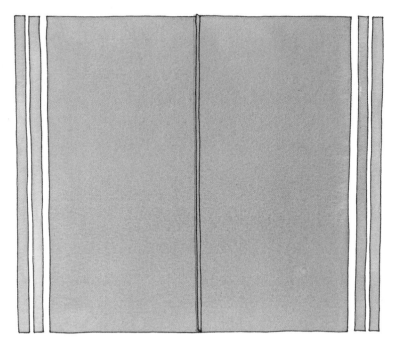

3 Using a Hera marker and a quilter's quarter, mark the quilting lines ¼ in (0.75 cm) outside of all the stars and the same amount inside the centres. Mark straight lines around the borders, 3 in (8 cm) and 5 in (13 cm) from the narrow striped border. Hand quilt along the marked lines (**diagram 6**).

DIAGRAM 6

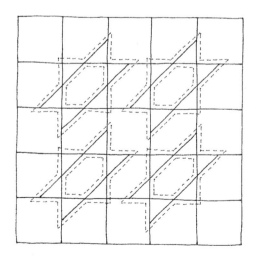

4 Trim the edges of the quilt and square up the corners. Using the binding strips, bind the edges of your quilt with a double straight binding.

"Economy 16-patch" Quilt

This simple 16-patch quilt has its roots in the 1930's, when resources were scarce. In those difficult times, the ability to sew small amounts of precious fabric into a lovely and useful quilt was a real bonus. Today this simple quilt allows you to be equally thrifty: you can showcase a selection of your favourite fabrics, yet have plenty of fabric left for future projects.

Finished size: 57½ x 57½ in (151 x 151 cm)

MATERIALS

All fabrics used in the quilt top are 45 in (115 cm) wide, 100% cotton

Coloured fabric in 16-patch block: 16 different prints, 10 in (.25 m) of each

Calico in 16-patch block: bleached calico, 1yd, 16 in (1.3 m)

Sashing and borders: print to coordinate with patches, 1⅔ yd (1.75 m)

Binding fabric: green floral fabric, 14 in (40 cm)

Backing fabric: 67½ x 67½ in (172 x 172 cm)

Wadding: cotton, 67½ x 67½ in (172 x 172 cm)

Rotary cutter, ruler and cutting mat

Markers: fabric pencil

Threads: sewing thread, white quilting thread

CUTTING

1 From the calico, cut the following:
- 16 strips 3 in (7.5 cm) wide.

2 From the printed coloured fabrics, cut the following:
- 1 strip 3 in (7.5 cm) wide from each.

3 From the sashing and border fabric, cut the following:
- 4 strips 3 in (7.5 cm) wide. Cross-cut these strips into 12 segments 10½ in (27 cm) long, trimming off any selvedges. Set these aside. Cut 4 more strips 3 in (7.5 cm) wide and set aside. For the border, cut 7 strips of fabric 5½ in (14 cm) wide. Set these aside.

4 From the binding fabric, cut the following:
- 6 strips 2¼ in (6 cm) wide. Set these aside.

STITCHING

1 Take the 16 strips of printed fabric and pair each one with a strip of calico. With the right sides together, sew along one long edge of the strip using a ¼ in (5 mm) seam allowance. Press the seam allowance towards the printed fabric. Repeat for the remaining 15 pairs of strips.

2 From the new strip of calico and printed fabric, trim off the selvedge and cross-cut the strip into eight 3 in (7.5 cm) sections. Repeat on the remaining 15 new strips.

QUILT PLAN

3 To sew a 16-patch block, take the eight sections of the strip and pair them into four-patch units, flipping the print and calico to form a checkerboard **(diagram 1)**. Place them right sides together, making sure the seam junctions fit snugly, and sew together. Now sew these units together in pairs, again flipping the calico and printed fabrics to con-

tinue the checkerboard effect **(diagram 2)**. Ensure that the seam junctions fit snugly together. Press all the seams in one direction.

4 Sew the two rows together to complete the checkerboard effect, again ensuring the seam junctions fit snugly together and pressing the long seam in one direction **(diagram 3)**. Repeat this process for the remaining fifteen blocks and set aside.

5 Following the quilt plan above, set out your blocks in a pleasing arrangement with four rows of four squares, ensuring that all blocks have a printed fabric square in the top left-hand corner. When you are happy with the arrangement, sew the blocks into rows by adding the short sashing strips **(diagram 4)**.

DIAGRAM 1   DIAGRAM 2

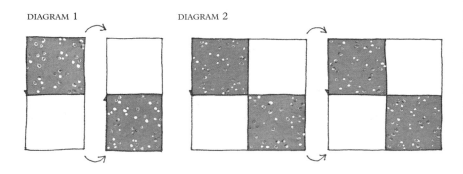

DIAGRAM 3

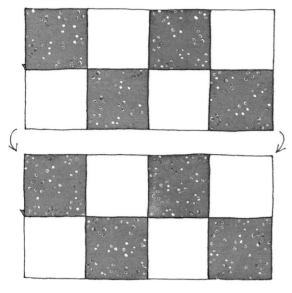

Pin and sew for accuracy, pressing all seams to the sashing fabric. Now take the long sashing strips, trim off the selvedge, and join them along their short ends to make one long strip. Press the seams open. Using the tape measure, measure and cut the strip into three lengths, each measuring 48 in (124.5 cm). Sew each of the three lengths between a row of blocks, using pins to ensure accuracy. Press all seams to the long sashes.

7 Trim the selvedge off of the four remaining border strips. Join the strips along their short edges to make two long strips. Press the seams open. Mark and cut each long strip to measure 58 in (151.5 cm). Pin and sew these strips to the top and bottom of the quilt. Press the seams towards the border fabric.

FINISHING

1 Lay the backing, right side down, on a large flat surface with the wadding on top. Centre the quilt, right side up, over the backing and wadding. Carefully smooth all three layers, making sure there are no wrinkles. Using a long needle and a light coloured thread, tack the layers together.

2 Traditionally, the design of this quilt was marked freehand, but for your convenience, a template is given on page 92 for you to mark on the quilt to as shown (**diagram 5**). Once you have quilted the marked outside curve, continue to fill in the arc with evenly spaced quilted lines.

3 Trim the edges of the quilt and square up the corners. Using the binding strips, bind the edges with a double straight binding with mitred corners.

DIAGRAM 4

DIAGRAM 5

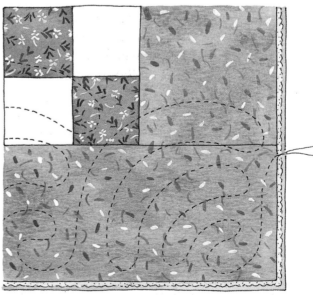

6 Take three strips of the border fabric and trim off the selvedges. Sew the strips together along the short ends to create one long strip. Press the seams open. Mark and cut the strip into two lengths, each measuring 48 in (124.5 cm) long. Pin and sew these lengths along the opposite sides of the quilt. Press the seams towards the border fabric.

Half-square Triangle Techniques

Here's another way to piece half-square triangle blocks from squares. It's quick and accurate – even for beginners. All you have to do is stitch along the lines before cutting the triangles apart.

QUICK HALF-SQUARE UNITS

This is such a foolproof way of piecing half-square triangle blocks that you will want to use it again and again. Squares are cut to the appropriate size and stitched before cutting the triangles.

First determine the size of the triangles you wish to cut, and then work out the size of the square which you will need by adding $\frac{7}{8}$ in (2.5 cm) to the finished measurement of the short side of the triangle. Each square will result in two finished triangles; therefore, if the pattern calls for ten red triangles paired with ten white triangles, you would only need to cut five squares of each colour. On the back of the lighter of the two squares, draw a diagonal line from corner to corner. This is the cutting line. Draw the stitching lines $\frac{1}{4}$ in (0.75 cm) on either side of the diagonal. Place the light and dark squares right sides together and pin to hold them in place. Stitch along the seam lines on either side of the diagonal (**A**). Slice the squares in two along the cutting line (**B**). Press towards the darker of the two triangles, unless instructed otherwise (**C**) and snip off the "dog ears". Squares may be chain-pieced for even quicker results.

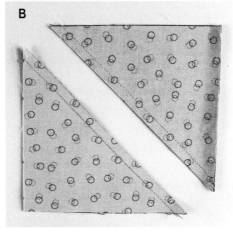

A

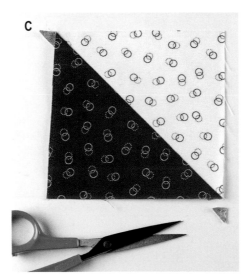

B

C

SEWING AND PRESSING MULTIPLE INTERSECTING SEAMS

In the pinwheel block used in the quilt on pages 50–54, pressing the seams to eliminate bulk where the eight seams intersect will become very important, and will take precedence over the usual rule of pressing towards the darker fabric. There are two ways to deal with this problem. In the first method, used where four half-square units join to form the block, the seams are pressed in a circular direction. In the second method, used in the corners of the quilt where four blocks meet, the seams are pressed open.

In the first method, when joining two half-square units, press the centre seam in the same circular direction as the two units (**D**). Pin the two halves of the block together with the central seam-points matching.

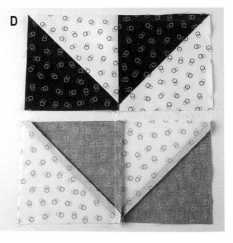

D

After stitching the two halves of the block together, use your seam ripper to unpick the central crossing seam within the seam allowance to enable all of the seams to be pressed in a circular fashion (**E**).

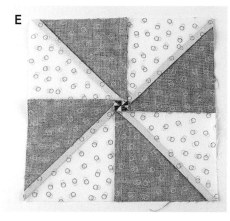

The second method, which is used where strips of blocks are stitched together, means that you won't have the option of circular pressing. The seams between the blocks will need to be pressed in alternate directions, and the long seams are, therefore, best pressed open (**F**).

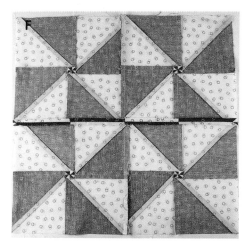

MAKING A TEMPLATE FOR A QUILTING PATTERN

Templates for marking quilting patterns do not need to be quite as accurate as those for piecing. Thin card, even that from a used cereal packet, will be adequate for marking an individual quilt top. Where a project gives you a template for a quilting pattern you will need to trace the patterns onto tracing or greaseproof paper. Cut out the paper pattern with a generous allowance around it. Glue it to a piece of card and cut out along the drawn lines. If you use a cereal packet, glue the pattern to the shiny side; the rough card side will help to keep your template from slipping when you are marking around it.

MARKING OUT A QUILTING PATTERN

The cable pattern used on the inner border of the following quilt is used as an example. Find the midpoint of the border and mark a line with straight pins along its length. Begin drawing the cable pattern at the seam line (**diagram 1**) with the end points of the cable along the line marked by the pins. In this case the length of the cable is the same as the half-square unit so you will be able to fit six repeats along the top and bottom borders and eight along the sides. You may have to stretch or shrink the cable slightly to make it fit. Hold the template in place and use a marking pencil or Hera marker to mark a crease line around the template each time. Mark all four sides of the border first, and then position the second template to complete the corners.

DIAGRAM 1

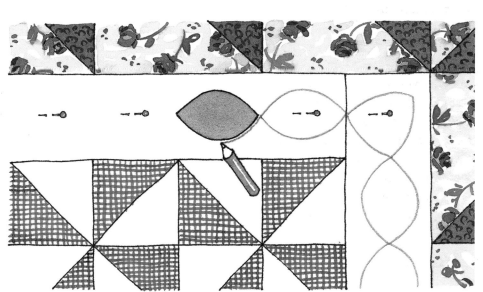

"Country Squire's Medallion" Quilt

This cheerful contemporary version of a very traditional old English medallion-style quilt gives you lots of practice piecing half-square triangles. Indeed, they form the only patchwork pattern in the quilt. A combination of machine quilting plus a single graceful hand quilted cable makes a speedy finish without sacrificing looks or style.

Finished size: 64 x 72 in (160 x 180 cm)

MATERIALS

All fabrics in the quilt top are 45 in (115 cm) wide, 100% cotton

Outer border and large triangles in middle border: rose-patterned fabric, 3 yds (2.75 m)

Small triangles and first border: White-on-cream printed fabric, 1⅔ yds (1.5 m)

Small triangles and binding: green mini-check, 1⅔ yds (1.5 m)

Large triangles in middle border: dark pink fabric, 1⅛ yds (1.1 m)

Backing fabric: 4¼ yds (3.9 m)

Wadding: 100% cotton, 68 x 76 in (180 x 200 cm)

Rotary cutter, ruler and cutting mat

Threads: thread for machine and hand quilting

Markers: fabric marking pencil, Hera marker

Tracing or greaseproof paper, glue stick, thin card, paper scissors

CUTTING

1 From the main rose-patterned fabric, cut the following:

● one length 60 in (150 cm) long. Cut four strips 8½ in (21.5 cm) wide down the length of the fabric, avoiding the selvedges. Trim two of these strips to a finished length of 56½ in (141.5 cm). Trim the other two to a finished length of 48½ in (121.5 cm). Set these aside for the outer borders.

● three strips 8⅞ in (22.5 cm) deep across the width of the fabric. From each strip cut four 8⅞ in (22.5 cm) squares giving you a total of twelve. Discard one and set the remaining eleven aside.

2 From the white-on-cream fabric, cut the following:

● four strips 4½ in (11.5 cm) deep across the width of the fabric. Trim each strip to a length of 32½ in (81.5 cm), avoiding the selvedges, and set aside for the inner borders.

● four strips 4⅞ in (12.5 cm) deep. Cross-cut each strip into eight 4⅞ in (12.5 cm) squares, avoiding the selvedges.

3 From the green mini-check fabric, cut the following:

● four strips 4⅞ in (12.5 cm) deep. Cross-cut each strip into eight 4⅞ in (12.5 cm) squares, avoiding the selvedges.

● eight strips 2½ in (6 cm) deep across the width of the fabric. Set aside for the binding.

QUILT PLAN

4 From the dark pink fabric, cut the following:

● three strips 8⅞ in (22.5 cm) deep across the width of the fabric. Cross-cut each strip into four 8⅞ in (22.5 cm) squares. Discard one square and set the rest aside.

5 Divide the backing fabric into two lengths of 76 in (195 cm). Remove the selvedges.

STITCHING

1 On the back of each of the 32 cream squares draw a diagonal line from corner to corner. Mark a line ¼ in (0.75 cm) on either side of the diagonal. Place one cream square on a green check square, right sides together, carefully aligning all four sides. Pin and stitch the seam lines on either side of the diagonal. Cut along the drawn diagonal and press the seams towards the darker fabric on each set of triangles. Repeat for the remaining 31 squares.

2 Stitch the squares together in pairs. Press the seams towards the cream fabric this time. Now stitch the two halves of the block together, carefully pinning and matching the two centre seams. Press this final seam in a circular direction, unpicking crossing seam allowances where necessary.

3 Stitch three blocks together to form a row. Repeat three more times. Press these short seams in alternate directions for each row. Stitch the rows together, pinning to align seam junctions. Press these seams open **(diagram 1)**.

DIAGRAM 1

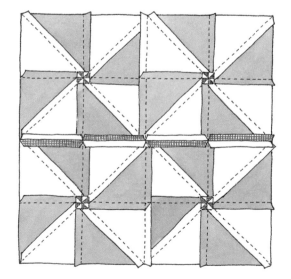

4 Stitch a cream strip to both sides of the centre medallion. Add the remaining two strips to the top and bottom. Press all seams towards the cream border strips.

5 Mark the back of the rose print squares (or whichever of your fabrics is the lighter) in the same way as the cream squares. Layer a rose print square and a dark pink square, right sides together. Pin and stitch. Cut apart and press towards the darker fabric. Repeat for all the squares.

6 Set aside two of these large half-square triangle blocks for the moment, and stitch together four strips of five blocks each. Stitch the remaining two blocks to the left-hand end of two of the strips, turning the block in the opposite direction before doing so **(diagram 2)**.

DIAGRAM 2

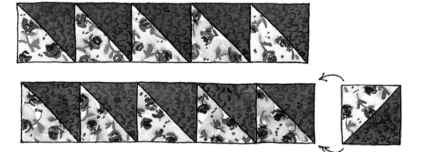

7 Following the quilt plan, pin and stitch the two short strips to the sides of the quilt. Press the seams towards the border. Pin and stitch the top and bottom borders in place, taking care to position them correctly. Press as before.

8 Stitch a cream and green check block to either end of the two 48½ in (121.5 cm) long border strips, pressing seams towards the border strip.

9 Fold and mark the centre of the 56½ in (141.5 cm) long border strips with a pin. Matching the centre points, stitch a border strip to either side of the quilt. Press towards the border strip. Stitch the top and bottom borders, with cream and green check blocks attached, to the top and bottom of the quilt. Press towards the border strips.

FINISHING

1 Stitch the two lengths of backing fabric together down the long seam. Press the seam to one side. Trim the backing fabric so that it is 2 in (5 cm) larger all around than the quilt top. Trim the wadding to the same size as the backing fabric.

2 Place the backing fabric, right side down, on a flat surface. Place the wadding on top. Centre the quilt, right side up, over the wadding and backing, taking care to ensure that there are no wrinkles. Pin over the surface of the quilt, using safety pins.

3 Prepare your quilting templates (see page 90) and mark the inner cream border.

4 Following the quilting diagram **(diagram 4)**, use a Hera marker to mark the straight quilting lines.

5 Machine quilt round the blocks and in diagonal lines on the outer borders, using your walking foot attachment. Hand quilt the cable in the inner border.

6 Trim the outer edges of the quilt and square up the corners.

7 Join the eight binding strips together, on the bias, to form a continuous binding. Press the binding in half down its length. Use to bind the edges of the quilt, forming mitres at the corners as you go.

DIAGRAM 4

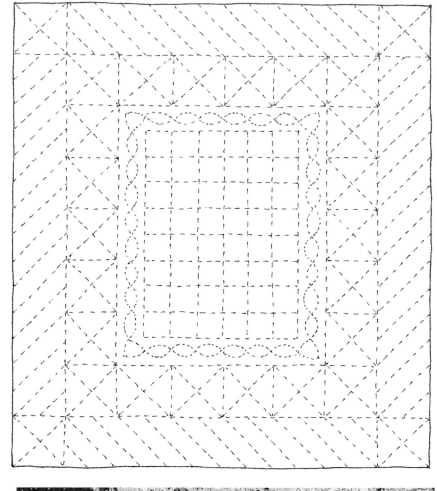

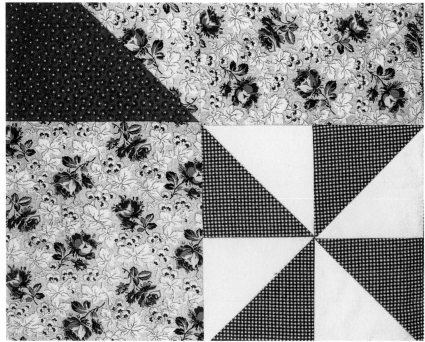

Easy Piecing Techniques

Some patchwork patterns look remarkably complicated, but when you know the secrets of these easy piecing techniques, you will have no problems putting them together.

PARTIAL PIECING

This technique is just a clever way of avoiding set-in angles. If you look at the diagram of block A in the quilt on page 58, you will see that it is composed of a centre square surrounded by four strips of equal lengths. Starting from the top of the block, attach the first strip to the centre square with a partial seam, which starts roughly in the centre of the square, so that the right-hand end is stitched and the left-hand end is loose (**A**). Fingerpress the partial seam towards the strip. Working clockwise around the centre

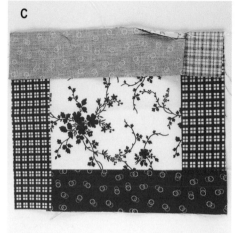

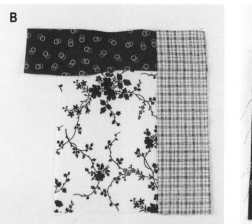

square, attach the second strip (**B**). This time the pieces should fit together evenly. Press the seam towards the strip. Add the third and fourth strips in a similar fashion, taking care to keep the loose end of the first strip out of the way (**C**). Finally, go back to the first strip and finish stitching the rest of the seam (**D**). Press towards the strip to complete the block (**E**).

BAGGING OUT

The quilt that follows on pages 56–59 does not have a separate binding. It is layered and stitched around four sides, leaving a gap in one side for turning. This is known as bagging out.

To bag out a quilt, spread your wadding out on a large flat surface, making sure it is wrinkle-free. Place the backing fabric centrally on top of the wadding, right side up. Place the quilt on top of the backing, right sides together. Smooth out any wrinkles and pin securely through all three layers around the outside edges.

Starting and ending with a couple of backstitches, stitch around the outside edges through all three layers with the wadding side down, leaving an opening on one side of about 12–15 in (30–40 cm). Trim the excess wadding from around the edges.

Reach between the layers and turn the quilt right side out, then slip-stitch the opening closed. Roll the edges between your fingers to locate the seam line exactly along the edge and carefully smooth out the layers. Quilt or tie to keep everything from shifting.

"Arbour Roses" Quilt

This quilt shows how looks can be deceiving as it is really quite simple to create. The woven effect comes from alternating two simple blocks. The first one has a central square surrounded by four equal length strips and is quickly pieced, without any set-in angles at all. The second block has corner triangles made from squares.

Finished size: 54 x 54 in (135 x 135 cm)

MATERIALS

All fabrics in the quilt top are 45 in (115 cm) wide, 100% cotton

Trellis: two contrasting patterned fabrics in pink and blue, 1⅔ yds (1.5 m) of each

Background: large rose patterned fabric, 2 yds (1.9 m)

Wadding: lightweight (2 oz) polyester, 56 x 56 in (142 x 142 cm)

Backing fabric: 3¼ yds (3 m)

Rotary cutter, ruler and cutting mat

Fabric marking pencil

Threads: sewing thread to match your fabrics, clear invisible machine quilting thread, 2 skeins of stranded embroidery cotton

Large eye quilting or embroidery needle for tying

CUTTING

1 From one of the trellis fabrics, cut the following:

● two strips 2½ in (6.5 cm) wide down the length of the fabric, avoiding the selvedges. Trim both to 52½ in (131.5 cm) long and set aside.

● twelve strips 2½ in (6.5 cm) deep across the width of the fabric. Avoiding the selvedges, cross-cut three of these strips into 2½ in (6.5 cm) squares, ten from the first two strips and four from the third one.

● Cross-cut each of the remaining nine strips into three segments 8½ in (21.5 cm) long, avoiding the selvedges. Discard one segment and set the remaining 26 aside.

2 Cut the second trellis fabric in the same way as the first.

3 From the background fabric, cut the following:

● four strips across the width of the fabric 10½ in (26.5 cm) deep. Cross-cut each strip into three 10½ in (26.5 cm) squares, avoiding the selvedges. Either use a second ruler or the markings on your cutting mat for these wide strips.

● three more strips each 6½ in (16.5 cm) deep across the width of the fabric, avoiding the selvedges. Cross-cut these strips into 6½ in (16.5 cm) squares, five squares each from the first two strips and three from the third one. Set aside.

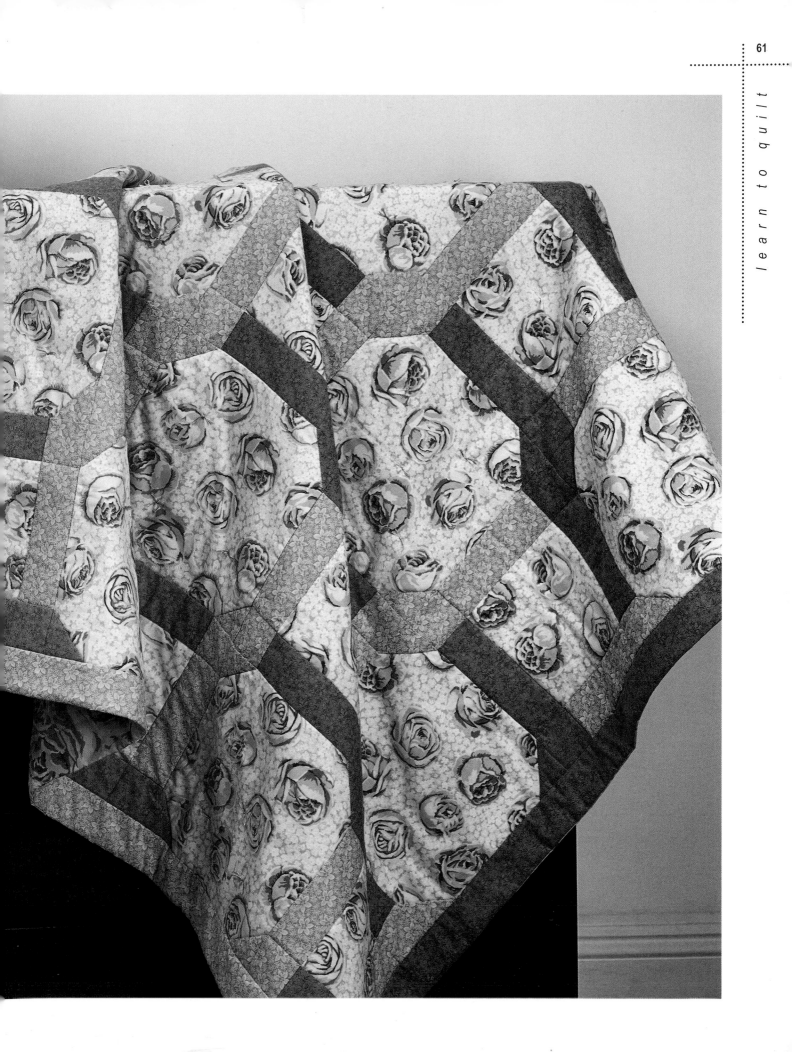

QUILT PLAN

4 Cut the backing fabric into two lengths of 56 in (140 cm). Trim off the selvedges.

STITCHING

1 This quilt is composed of two simple block patterns alternating across the quilt. Study the diagram of both blocks to familiarize yourself with them. There are 13 block As and 12 block Bs **(diagram 1)**.

2 Place the first pink strip along the top of a 6½ in (16.5 cm) square, right sides together,

DIAGRAM 1

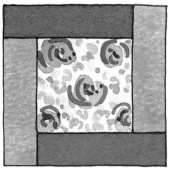

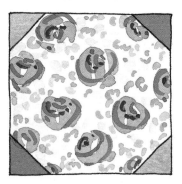

Block A (make 13)   Block B (make 12)

matching up the right-hand end of the strip with the corner of the square. Pin and partial piece the strip. Repeat this step for all the A blocks. Finger press the half-seam towards the strip. Turning the partially stitched block in an anti-clockwise direction, stitch a blue strip on next. This seam, and the next two, can be chain pieced. Press all seams towards the strips. Finally, go back and finish stitching the last half of the first seam. Press and set aside the completed block As.

3 Using a fabric marker, draw a single diagonal on the wrong side of the 24 2½ in (6.5 cm) pink and blue squares. Pin two pink squares in opposite corners of the large background squares, right sides together. Repeat for the blue ones in the remaining corners. Stitch along the drawn diagonals to form triangles. Press and trim away the excess fabric. Stitch all 12 block Bs like this.

4 Lay the completed blocks out following the quilt plan, opposite. Stitch the blocks together into five strips. Press all seams towards the partially pieced blocks. Pin the strips together, matching the seams between the blocks, and stitch. Press the long seams towards the bottom of the quilt.

5 Following the colour placement on the diagram, stitch the long border strips to the quilt using partial piecing. Press the seams towards the strips.

6 Stitch the two lengths of backing fabric together and press the seam towards one side.

FINISHING

1 Trim the backing fabric to the same size as the quilt top.

2 Bag out the quilt, then smooth the quilt layers and place safety pins over the surface to hold them together while quilting. Use invisible machine quilting thread on the top and a sewing thread to match your backing fabric in the bobbin. With the walking foot attachment on your sewing machine, quilt in the ditch along the lines of the trellis, starting and stopping ¼ in (0.75 cm) from the edge of the quilt. Stitch all around the quilt ¼ in (0.75 cm) from the outside edge.

3 Using the stranded embroidery cotton and a large-eye embroidery needle, tie the large unquilted areas within the trellis. Place a single tie in the centre of the square and place five ties in the octagon shape.

Foundation Piecing

You too can join the flock of knowledgeable quilters who have discovered that foundation piecing is a wonderful way of achieving very accurate results. And you won't even have to worry about cutting your patches accurately!

FOUNDATION PIECING

Foundation piecing requires a pattern for each block or unit, with each patch numbered according to the order in which it will be stitched. The fabrics for these patches are pinned to the reverse side of the foundation pattern, but are stitched along the lines on the pattern side. Once stitched, the patch is flipped over and fingerpressed in place ready for attaching the next patch. Because you are stitching along a drawn line each time, you end up with perfect points effortlessly.

I suggest you use ordinary greaseproof paper for foundation piecing. It is cheap, easy to obtain (you probably already have some in a kitchen drawer) and tears away easily. The only drawback is having to trace so many repeats of the pattern, so I usually alternate drawing and stitching to relieve the tedium. Use a fine-line permanent marker pen for tracing, fine-line for greater accuracy and permanent so that no ink will transfer to your fabrics. Be sure to include the numbers on your tracings, and the broken lines around the pattern to remind you of the outer seam allowance **(A)**.

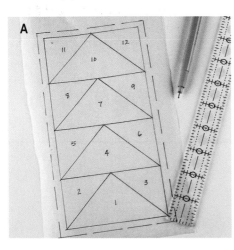

Unlike the usual patchwork method which demands accurate cutting, foundation patches are deliberately cut larger than you need. It's a very good way to use up leftover fabric, simply trimming it to size with scissors.

Take one foundation pattern and place it marked side down in front of you. Position the appropriate fabric, right side up, centrally over patch number 1 **(B)**. Make sure the fabric covers not only the patch but also at least $\frac{1}{4}$ in (0.75 cm) around all the edges. Pin it in place from the paper side.

Place it on your cutting mat with the foundation pattern uppermost. Fold the

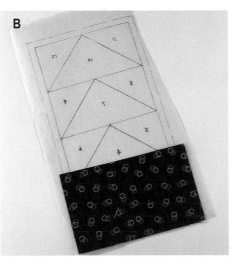

pattern back along the line between 1 and 2, position your rotary ruler with the $\frac{1}{4}$ in (0.75 cm) mark along the crease and trim the excess fabric back to the correct seam allowance **(C)**.

Turn the foundation pattern back over to the fabric side and place the appropriate patch over the first one, right sides together, using the trimmed edge of the first fabric as a guide. As before, check to make sure your

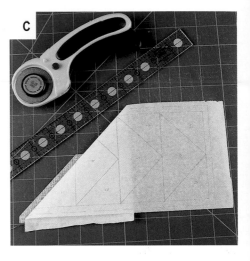

NOTE:

If you pin the first patch in place temporarily along the seam line and flip it up, you will be able to check its correct position at a glance. Re-pin the patch in place from the paper side so you can see the pin when stitching.

fabric will cover all of the patch area and extend far enough outwards to cover the seam allowances on all of its sides.

Place the foundation and patches under the presser foot, pattern side up, and stitch along the line between patches 1 and 2 using a stitch length that is only slightly shorter than normal. Start and finish a stitch or two past the ends of the line. Cut the threads **(D)**.

D

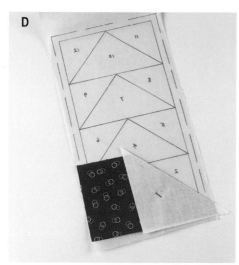

Flip patch 2 back and fingerpress it in place, using a pin to hold it. Turn the foundation to the paper side, fold the paper back along the line between 2 and 3 and trim the seam allowance. Position patch 3, right side down, using the cut edge as a guide. Pin from the paper side and stitch the seam between 1 and 3 **(E)**. Flip, fingerpress and pin.

E

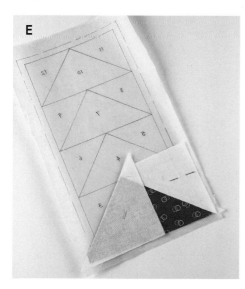

Turn over to the paper side and trim the seam allowance. You may have to pull the paper gently away from the stitches that run across the seam line in order to be able to fold on the line. Continue adding patches in sequence to the foundation pattern until it is complete **(F and G)**, then trim the seam allowances of the whole foundation unit to the usual $\frac{1}{4}$ in (0.75 cm).

F

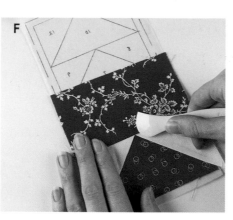

G

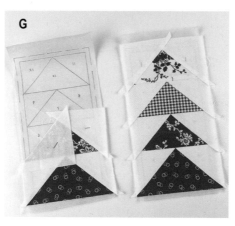

Stitch the required number and use in the normal way as specified in your quilt project. Once all the patches are stitched together, you can remove the foundation papers **(H)**. Greaseproof paper pulls away easily, but you may find that a pair of tweezers is helpful in awkward spots. Strips of sticky tape wound around your hand and lightly rolled across the back of the patchwork should help to pick up the last stray bits of paper.

H

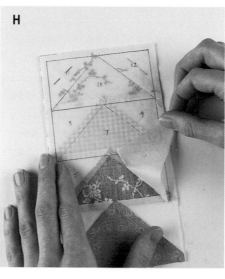

Remember these basic pointers for trouble-free foundation piecing.

1 Cut the patches generously large.

2 The pattern is drawn on one side of the foundation paper and the fabrics are stitched to the opposite side.

3 The first patch is always positioned right side up and all the rest are positioned right side down.

4 Fold the paper out of the way and trim the previously stitched seam allowance to form a guide for accurate placement of the next patch.

5 Trim outer seam allowances when the stitching is complete.

6 Remove the foundation paper pattern after all sides have been stitched in a seam or have been stay-stitched.

WORKING WITH STRIPES

Using stripes and other directional fabrics can add vitality and interest to your patchwork. In the quilt which follows, the multi-coloured stripe was not only the inspiration for the colour scheme, but also determined the width of the sashing strips. When using a striped fabric, you may have to alter the measurements within your quilt to suit. Don't forget to take that into account when you are calculating your fabric amounts. Study the pattern to decide how many repeats you can get out of a width (most stripes run parallel to the selvedges), not forgetting to take the seam allowances into account. You will have to cut each strip individually. With care, you may be able to cut with your rotary cutter, otherwise use your fabric scissors and the stripes to guide you.

"Join the Flock" Quilt

The pattern in this project, a traditional one known as Flying Geese, is set in long vertical columns. It is perfect for showing off a striped fabric in the sashes. The width of the sashing can be adjusted to fit the size of any striped repeat so don't be afraid to experiment!

Finished size: 32 x 44 in (80 x 110 cm)

MATERIALS

All fabrics used in the quilt top are 45 in (115 cm) wide, 100% cotton

Vertical sashing and outer border: bright pastel stripe, 1⅓ yds (1.25 m)

"Geese" and binding: four bright textured pastel fabrics, 23 in (60 cm) of each fabric

Background triangles: plain white fabric, 1⅓ yds (1.25 m)

Backing fabric: 1⅓ yds (1.25 m)

Wadding: 100% cotton, 34 x 46 in (85 x 115 cm)

Rotary cutter, ruler and cutting mat

Greaseproof paper, fine-line permanent marker pen, scissors

Thread: sewing thread, machine quilting thread

Straight pins, safety pins, sharps needle

Fabric spray adhesive

PREPARATION AND CUTTING

1 Trace off 25 foundation patterns (see Templates, page 92 for imperial and page 93 for metric) onto greaseproof paper using a ruler and a fine-line permanent marker pen. Don't forget to number the patches.

NOTE:
Because each column of flying geese has a different colour sequence, you may find it helpful to write the name of the colour of each of the "geese" on the foundation with pencil. Instead of putting it on the pattern side, write it on the opposite side so you can read it when you position the fabrics. I suggest you complete one column at a time so that all the units you are working on will have the same sequence. The diagrams show the position of the different fabrics and how many to make of each unit.

QUILT PLAN

Column A   Column B   Column C   Column D   Column E

2 **From each of the four textured pastel fabrics, cut the following:**

● four strips 3 in (8 cm) deep across the width of the fabric. Cross-cut the strips into segments 5 in (13 cm) long, avoiding the selvedges. You need 25 of each colour. Set aside.

● one strip 2½ in (6.5 cm) deep across the width of the fabric from each of the four fabrics. Trim off the selvedges and set aside for the binding.

3 **From the plain white fabric, cut the following:**

● ten strips 3½ in (9 cm) deep across the width of the fabric. Cross-cut each strip into ten 3½ in (9 cm) squares, avoiding the selvedges. Slice all the squares in half once diagonally to give you 200 half-square triangles, and set aside.

4 **From the striped fabric, cut the following:**

● eight strips 2½ in (6.5 cm) wide down the length of the fabric, avoiding the selvedges. Trim six of these down to 40½ in (101.5 cm) long. Trim the remaining two to 32½ in (81.5 cm) long and set all of them aside.

> **NOTE:**
> **You may have to adjust these measurements to suit the dimensions of the striped fabric you have chosen. Remember to make any necessary adjustments to backings, wadding and binding also.**

STITCHING

1 Study the quilt plan, opposite, and the different units needed for each column (**diagram 1**) and note that each column is made up of a certain number of units: Column A uses 5 x Unit A, Column B uses 5 x Unit B, Column C uses 5 x Unit C, Column D uses 5 x Unit D and Column E

DIAGRAM 1

Unit A (make 10)   Unit B (make 5)   Unit C (make 5)   Unit D (make 5)

uses 5 x Unit A. Foundation piece all of the units for one column and stitch them together. Repeat for the other four.

2 Stitch a striped sashing to the left-hand side of each pieced column, pinning and matching mid- and quarter-points on each one. Add the final sash to the right-hand side of the last column. Stitch the columns and sashes together, and press all the seams towards the sashes. Stitch the last two strips to the top and bottom of the quilt. Press the seams towards the strips.

3 Remove all foundation papers.

FINISHING

1 Using the spray adhesive, layer the quilt and place a few safety pins in it to hold it together while quilting.

2 Using the walking foot attachment on your sewing machine, machine quilt in the ditch around each column.

3 Square up the corners, and trim away the excess backing and wadding.

4 Join the four pastel strips to form a continuous binding, and use to bind the edges of the quilt, mitring the corners as you go.

"Which One Shall I Wear Today?" Quilt

This quilt, with its Bow Tie blocks, is a good one to make for a man or boy. The traditional method for piecing this block requires set-in angles, four per block, but we know an easier way. Using triangles from squares, you'll soon be reeling in the compliments.

Finished size: 65½ x 65½ in (163 x 163 cm)

MATERIALS

All fabrics used in the quilt top are 45 in (115 cm) wide, 100% cotton

Bow ties: five bright coloured fabrics in different patterns, one long quarter yard/metre for each

Background: seven different but toning shades of plain blue fabric, ⅞ yd (80 cm) of each

Border and backing: plain blue (you can repeat one of the background fabrics or choose an eighth shade), 3⅞ yds (3.5 m)

Binding: one of the tie fabrics, ⅔ yd (60 cm)

Wadding: 100% cotton or polycotton blend, 70 x 70 in (177 x 177 cm)

Rotary cutter, ruler and cutting mat

Thread: sewing thread, multi-colour machine quilting thread

75 small shirt buttons

CUTTING

1 From one of the tie fabrics, cut the following:

● one strip 3½ in (9 cm) deep across the width of the fabric. Cross-cut into ten 3½ in (9 cm) squares, avoiding the selvedges.

● one strip 1½ in (3.75 cm) deep across the width of the fabric. Cross-cut into ten 1½ in (3.75 cm) squares, avoiding the selvedges.

Draw a diagonal line on the back of each of these squares.

● Repeat for each of the tie fabrics.

2 From one of the plain blue background fabrics, cut the following:

● one strip 9¼ in (23 cm) deep across the width of the fabric. Cross-cut into four 9¼ in (23 cm) squares, avoiding the selvedges.

● two more strips 5⅛ in (13.1 cm) deep across the width of the fabric. Cross-cut one strip into seven 5⅛ in (13.1 cm) squares, avoiding the selvedges. Remove the selvedges from the second strip and cut one more 5⅛ in (13.1 cm) square. Reduce the depth of the remainder of the strip to 3½ in (9 cm), then cross-cut eight 3½ in (9 cm) squares from it. Slice these eight squares once diagonally to give 16 half-square triangles.

● Repeat for each of the plain blue background fabrics. You will have some extra patches to allow you to play with different combinations.

3 Divide the backing fabric into two equal lengths and remove the selvedges from both lengths. Cut two strips 3½ in (9 cm) wide down the length of each piece of backing fabric. Set these aside to be used for the borders.

4 From the binding fabric, cut the following:

● seven strips 2½ in (6 cm) deep across the width of the fabric. Remove the selvedges and set aside.

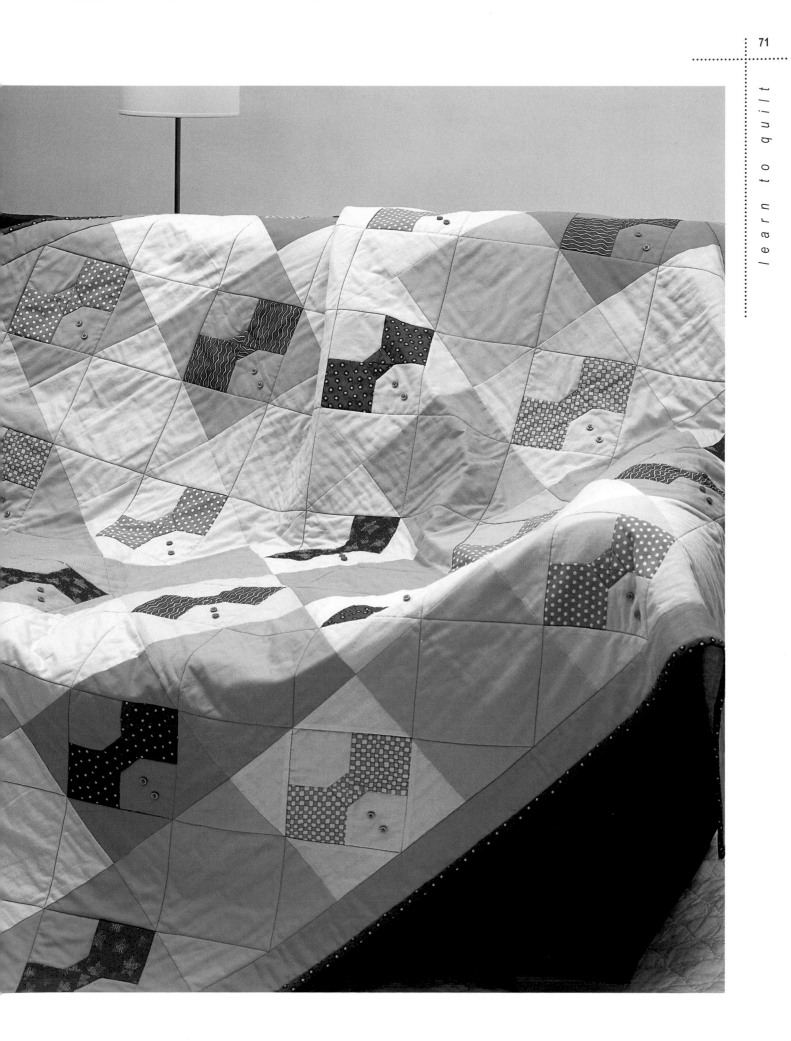

QUILT PLAN

STITCHING

1 Each Bow Tie block is composed of the tie plus two background patches. Corner triangles are added to set the block on point. For each of the 25 blocks you will need two large and two small squares from a tie fabric, and two 3½ in (9 cm) squares plus four half-square triangles from a plain blue background fabric. Decide on the different combinations and stack them together.

2 To construct one Bow Tie block, place a small tie square in the corner of a blue square, right sides together and matching the outer corners. Pin and stitch along the line.

Flip and press towards the tie fabric to enhance the three-dimensional effect. Repeat. Trim away the excess fabric from the fabrics underneath the triangles. Your block is now, essentially, a simple four-patch which you stitch together in the normal way **(diagram 1)**.

3 Fold the corner triangles to mark the centre point of the long (diagonal) side. Stitch one to each side of the four-patch block, pressing towards the triangle after each addition. Repeat for all 25 blocks, then square up the corners and trim all the blocks to the same size.

DIAGRAM 1

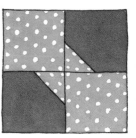

4 Lay out the Bow Tie blocks alternating with plain blue squares. It doesn't matter if the same fabrics touch each other. When you are happy with your arrangement, pin an identifying number or letter on each row. Pin and stitch the blocks into horizontal strips. Press all seams in each strip towards the plain squares. This will ensure that the seams interlock. Pin and stitch the long strips together, matching the short seams. Press the long seams towards the bottom of the quilt.

5 Measure vertically through the centre of your quilt and cut two of the border strips to that length. Mark the midpoints and quarter-points of both quilt and border strips. Matching the points, pin and stitch the borders to the sides of the quilt. Press the seams towards the border strips.

6 Measure the width of your quilt horizontally through the centre, including the side borders. Mark, pin and stitch the top and bottom borders in the same way as the side borders. Press towards the border strips.

7 Mark, pin and stitch the two lengths of backing fabric together down the long seam. Press the seam allowance to one side.

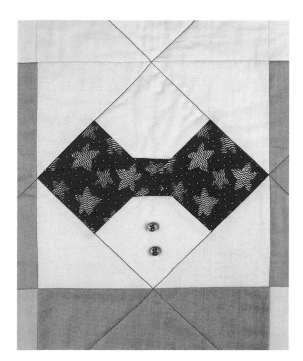

FINISHING

1 Smooth your backing fabric out, right side down, on a large flat surface. Place the wadding centrally over the backing, smoothing it into place. Place the quilt centrally on top of the wadding, right side down, and make sure there are no wrinkles in any of the layers. Pin the layers together with safety pins. Following the quilting lines, machine quilt the layers **(diagram 2)**.

DIAGRAM 2

2 Using your rotary cutter and ruler, trim the edges of your quilt, squaring up the corners as you go.

3 Stitch the binding strips together to form a continuous binding and use to bind the edges of your quilt, forming mitres at the corners.

> **NOTE:**
> **Do not use buttons on a quilt for a baby or small child. Instead, embroider any details you wish to include.**

"Hidden Stars" Quilt

Sew this quilt from scraps of your favourite colour – the more different fabrics, the better – but be sure to keep to one colour! There are no tricky triangles to cut, and the "cut and flip" method used ensures accuracy. Because of the diversity of fabrics used, and because they are all the same colour, the pattern creates the optical effect of an Ohio Star moving over the quilt.

Finished size: 60 x 60 in (152 x 152 cm)

MATERIALS

All fabrics used in the quilt top are 45 in (115cm) wide, 100% cotton

Main feature blue fabric: various blue fabrics, scraps to total 2 yds, 6 in (2.2 m) (You must be able to cut a square 6½ in (16 cm) from each scrap)

Alternate fabric: bleached calico, 2 yds, 6 in (2.2 m)

Border: four different blue fabrics (preferably fabrics that have been used in the quilt), 15 in (40 cm) of each

Binding: one of the blue fabrics, 15 in (40 cm)

Backing fabric: 70 x 70 in (178 x 178 cm)

Wadding: 100% cotton, 70 x 70 in (178 x 178 cm)

Rotary cutter, ruler and cutting mat

Markers: fabric marking pencil, Hera marker

Masking tape, ¼ in (5mm) wide

Threads: sewing thread, quilting thread to match calico

CUTTING

1 From the blue fabrics, cut the following:

● six strips 6½ in (16 cm) wide. Cross-cut each strip into 6½ in (16 cm) squares. You will need 32 of these. Be sure to cut from a good selection of fabrics.

● 11 strips 3½ in (8 cm) wide, trimming off the selvedges. Cross-cut each strip into 3½ in (8 cm) squares. You will need 128 of these. Make sure you have cut from a good selection of fabrics. On the wrong side of these squares, use your ruler and marking pencil to draw a diagonal line from corner to corner. Set aside.

2 From the calico, cut the following:

● six strips 6½ in (16 cm) wide, trimming off the selvedges. Cross-cut each strip into 6½ in (16 cm) squares. You will need 32 of these.

● 11 strips 3½ in (8 cm) wide, trimming off the selvedges. Cross-cut each strip into 3½ in (8 cm) squares. You will need 128 of these. On the wrong side of these squares, draw a diagonal line from corner to corner. Set aside.

3 From the blue fabric for the border, cut the following:

● two strips from four different blue fabrics 6½ in (16 cm) wide, trimming off the selvedges. Set these aside.

4 From the binding fabric, cut the following:

● 7 strips 2¼ in (5.5 cm) wide. Set aside.

QUILT PLAN

STITCHING

1 To sew the blocks with dark centres, collect the large blue squares and the small calico squares. Place a calico square wrong-side up in the top left-hand corner of a large blue square, right sides together. Ensure that the drawn line on the calico square runs from one side of the blue square to the top side **(diagram 1)**. Now sew along the drawn line. Repeat this process on the opposite corner of the large blue square **(diagram 2)**.

DIAGRAM 1

DIAGRAM 2

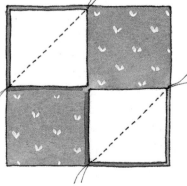

2 Using your ruler and rotary cutter, trim off the corner triangles ¼ in (0.5 cm) from the sewing line. Fold the triangles back to re-form the original square. Press the seam allowance towards the blue fabric **(diagram 3).**

DIAGRAM 3

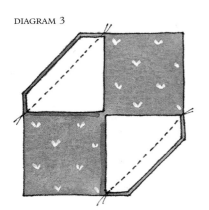

3 Repeat this process on the remaining two corners. When you have finished, all the corners that were originally blue should now be white **(diagram 4)**. Repeat this process using all of the blue squares to make 32 of these blocks.

DIAGRAM 4

4 To sew the blocks with white centres, collect the large calico squares and the small blue small squares. Repeat the process explained in steps 1-3 above, again making 32 of these blocks. If possible, use four different blues on each calico square, as this will maximize the optical effect of the Ohio Star block that will come and go when the quilt is complete. When pressing the seams, press towards the blue corner triangles, as this will help to ensure accuracy when assembling the quilt top.

5 Following the quilt plan, opposite, lay the blocks out on a flat surface (use the floor if this is convenient). Start with a dark-centred block in the top left-hand corner and place a light-centred block next to it, continuing along the row alternating blocks. Begin the second row with a light-centred block and again, continue along the row alternating blocks. Build up eight rows in this way using eight blocks per row. Keep building up the top of the quilt in this way until you have used all of the blocks.

6 Sew the blocks together row by row. As you sew, the blocks should fit neatly together, and the points should all match because of the way you pressed the blocks. Once the first row is sewn, press the seams towards the blocks with the light centres. Continue to press towards these blocks when sewing the rest of the rows, as this will help the straight seams sit together snugly, and your points will all match because of the previous pressing technique.

7 When all of the rows are completed and pressed, sew them together starting at the top of the quilt and working down. When sewing the first two rows together, insert a pin at each straight seam junction and where the points meet **(diagram 5)**. Again, the points and seams should easily match because of the pressing. When all of the rows are sewn together, press all seams in one direction.

DIAGRAM 5

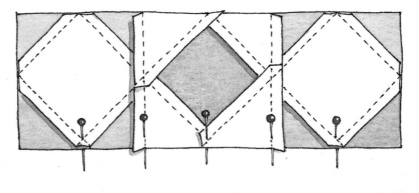

8 Take two strips of the same border fabric and sew them together along the short ends to form one long strip. Press the seam open. Repeat with the remaining border strips. Select the first two borders to be sewn on and place them on opposite sides of the quilt. Trim each of the long strips to measure 48½ in (123 cm) in length. Pin and sew the borders to the opposite sides of the quilt, pressing the seams towards the border. Now measure the remaining two strips and cut to 60½ in (151 cm). Pin and sew in place, pressing the seams to the border.

FINISHING

1 Lay the backing fabric right side down on a large flat surface with the wadding on top. Centre the quilt, right-side up, over the backing and wadding. Carefully smooth all three layers, making sure there are no wrinkles. Using a long needle and a light coloured thread, tack the quilt layers together.

2 Using the ¼ in (5 mm) masking tape, mark out three or four Ohio Stars at random places on the quilt, ¼ in (5 mm) in from the seams. Hand-quilt the pattern along the marked lines. Now, using the template on page 90, cover the remainder of the quilt with the flower motif **(diagram 6)**.

3 Mark a straight line inside the border ¼ in (5 mm) away from the seam to frame the centre of the quilt. Using a ruler and Hera marker, mark parallel lines 1 in (2.5 cm) apart at a 45° angle, stretching the width of the border **(diagram 6)**. Hand-quilt along the marked lines.

4 Trim the edges of the quilt and square up the corners. Using the binding strips, bind the edges of your quilt with a double binding with mitred corners.

DIAGRAM 6

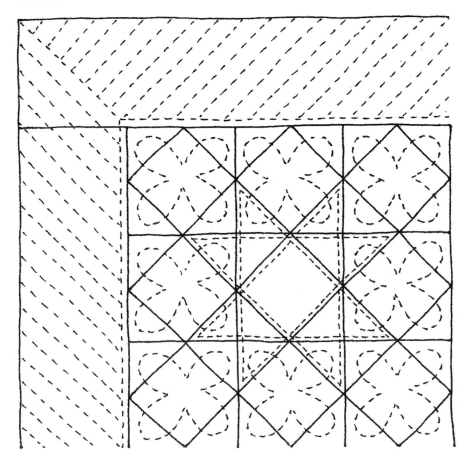

Making a Cushion Quilt

A quilt wrapped inside a pocket to make a cushion is such an unexpected yet practical idea with a myriad of uses. The fact that it can be adapted to different block patterns, sewing abilities and timetables makes it a technique well worth knowing.

CONSTRUCTING A CUSHION QUILT

Prepare the quilt top first, if it is to be pieced. Next prepare the pocket. Place the wadding square down first, then add the backing square right side up and the cushion front right side down. Pin the layers. Taking the usual $\frac{1}{4}$ in (0.75 cm) seam allowance, stitch around three sides, leaving the fourth side unstitched. If your block is directional, then it is the top edge of the block which is left unstitched. Reach between the layers and turn right side out, squaring the corners and rolling the layers so that the seam line falls right on the edge. Do not turn the raw edges of the unstitched side under; simply baste the layers together just within the seam allowance. Quilt or tie the pocket as desired.

Fold the top edge of the quilt backing to find the midpoint. With the backing fabric right side up and the pocket front side down, centre the pocket along the top edge of the backing. The basted edges of the pocket will be even with the raw edge of the fabric. Pin in place. Turn to the wrong side of the backing fabric and place two small squares of calico behind the lower corners of the pocket. Push a pin through from the other side to mark the exact location of the corner and centre the square over that. This helps reduce the strain on the backing fabric when the quilt is opened and closed. Attach the pocket to the backing fabric around three sides by stitching about $\frac{3}{16}$ in (4 mm) from the edge. The natural inclination is to leave the side which is the top of the cushion unstitched, but it is the bottom edge which must remain open.

To assemble the cushion quilt, spread the wadding out on a large flat surface. Next, centre the quilt backing, with attached cushion pocket, in the middle of the wadding, right side up. Place the quilt, right side down, on top, lining up the midpoints of the quilt and the cushion and having the top edges of both of them even. The cushion pocket will be sandwiched between the layers. Pin the layers securely, placing some pins in the body of the quilt to keep it from shifting. Trim the backing and wadding even with the edges of the quilt. Stitch around all four sides of the quilt, leaving an opening of about 15–18 in (40–45 cm) at the bottom. Reach between the backing and the front of the quilt, grasp the corners and turn the quilt right side out, squaring the corners and rolling the layers so that the seam line is on the edge of the quilt. Slip stitch the opening closed. Tie the quilt. In order to keep from tying the pocket shut, I slip the quilt pocket over the end of my ironing board while tying the area of the quilt that lies behind it.

FOLDING THE CUSHION QUILT

Follow the sequence of photographs **A–D**, right. Lay the quilt right side up with the pocket underneath and fold the sides of the quilt towards the middle, lengthways, even with the sides of the pocket. Reach inside the pocket and, grasping the edges of the folded quilt, turn the pocket right side out leaving the lower part of the quilt extending outward from the pocket. Fold the quilt up to the pocket and tuck it inside.

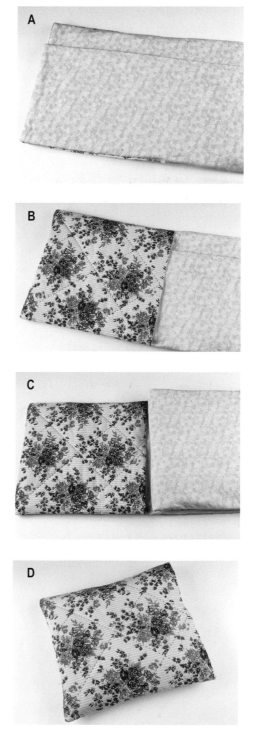

A

B

C

D

"Surprise Package" Quilt

I have seized this last opportunity to include a favourite pattern of mine, the basic nine-patch, and make no apologies for its simplicity. Indeed, I hope you have discovered from the quilts in this book that you don't have to use overly complicated patterns to achieve stunning results. Both the pocket and the quilt could even be made from a single wonderful piece of fabric for a quick, but very special, gift.

Finished size: 42 x 54 in (105 x 135 cm)

MATERIALS

All fabrics used are 45 in (115 cm wide), 100% cotton

Large squares and cushion front: bright floral pattern, 1⅓ yds (1.2 m) plus one fat quarter

Small squares, which form the "chain": bright contrasting mini-print fabric, 1¼ yds (1.2 m)

Alternate small squares: tone-on-tone floral to blend with main fabric, 1⅛ yds (1 m)

Backing for quilt and cushion pocket: 1⅔ yds (1.5 m) plus one fat quarter

Wadding: lightweight (2 oz) polyester, 44 x 56 in (110 x 140 cm) plus a square 18 x 18 in (45 x 45 cm)

Calico: two small pieces, each about 2 in (5 cm) square

Rotary cutter, ruler and cutting mat

Thread: sewing thread, coton à broder no.16, 2 skeins

Sashiko needle

Straight pins, safety pins

CUTTING

1 From the bright floral fabric, cut the following:

● six strips 6½ in (16.5 cm) deep across the width of the fabric. Cross-cut the first of these strips into six 6½ in (16.5 cm) squares, avoiding the selvedges, but you need only cut five from each of the remaining strips. Set these 31 squares aside. Trim the fat quarter for the cushion front to 16½ x 16½ in (42 x 42 cm).

2 From the bright mini-print fabric which will form the "chain", cut the following:

● 14 strips 2½ in (6.5 cm) deep across the width of the fabric. Trim off the selvedges, and cut each strip into two lengths of 20 in (50 cm).

3 From the tone-on-tone floral fabric, cut the following:

● 12 strips 2½ in (6.5 cm) deep across the width of the fabric. Trim off the selvedges, and cut each strip into two lengths of 20 in (50 cm).

4 Trim the fat quarter for the back of the cushion to 16½ x 16½ in (42 x 42 cm). Do not trim your quilt backing until you have finished piecing the quilt top.

QUILT PLAN

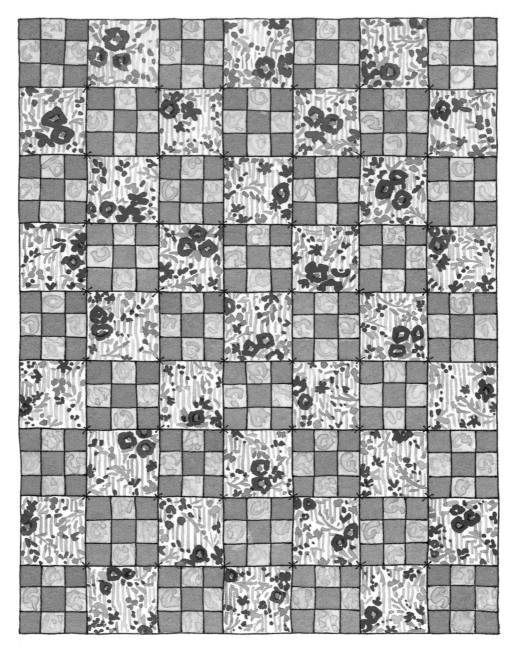

STITCHING

1 The nine-patch blocks are composed of two different strip sets. For set A, stitch a bright mini-print strip to either side of a tone-on-tone floral strip. Press the seams towards the darker fabric. Make eleven of these strip sets. For set B, stitch a tone-on-tone floral strip to either side of a bright mini-print strip . Press the seams towards the darker fabric. Make six of these strip sets **(diagram 1).**

DIAGRAM 1

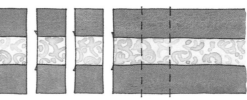

Strip set A

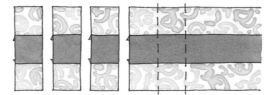

Strip set B

2 Cross-cut each strip set into six segments 2½ in (6.5 cm) wide. Stitch a strip set A to either side of a strip set B to make the nine patch blocks. Press the seams towards the bottom. Make 32 of these (**diagram 2**).

DIAGRAM 3

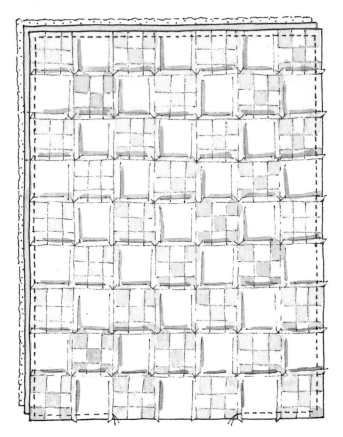

DIAGRAM 2

3 Study the quilt plan on page 72 and lay out the blocks in the correct order. Stitch all the blocks in each strip together. Press the seams towards the bright floral blocks. Stitch the strips together and press the seams towards the bottom of the quilt (**diagram 3**).

4 Layer the square of wadding, the pocket backing and pocket front. Pin and stitch around three sides. Trim the wadding to the same size as the pocket. Turn right side out and tack the top edge together. Quilt or tie the pocket.

DIAGRAM 4

5 Stitch the pocket to the backing fabric, reinforcing the corners of the cushion pocket (**diagram 4**).

6 Layer the wadding, backing with cushion pocket attached and the quilt front (**diagram 3**). Pin and stitch around the edges, leaving an opening at the bottom for turning. Trim away the excess wadding and square up the corners. Turn the quilt right side out and slip stitch the opening closed.

7 Smooth and place a few pins in the layers to keep them from slipping. Tie the quilt.

8 Fold the quilt up inside the cushion pocket.

Freestyle Quilting

If you are looking for a technique that is simple yet infinitely variable, where every quilt looks totally different with almost no effort on your part, then look no further. Designing a quilt specially to suit the recipient couldn't be easier.

CUTTING AND STITCHING ORIGINAL BLOCKS FROM STRIPS

To compare patchwork and quilting with cooking, this recipe is sure to please. It's easy, fat-free, and it will reduce your fabric stash at the same time! Furthermore, the result will be unique every time. Start by choosing several fabrics with a related theme (Christmas prints, animals, plaids – whatever you wish). Cut these fabrics into short strips of the same width but varying the lengths, avoiding the selvedges. Stitch all of the strips together, end to end, in a random fashion. Re-cut the resulting long length of stitched strips into similar sized sections and piece them into blocks.

Choose a width that suits the scale of the patterns you have chosen, or one that simply makes the most economical use of the amount of fabric you have. After cutting all the strips to this width, cross-cut them down into different lengths. You can either vary the lengths at random (**A**), or cut each strip down to two or three consistent lengths.

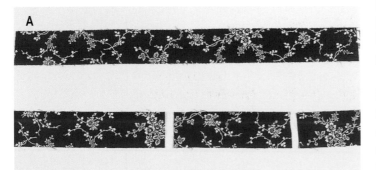

Randomly selecting different fabrics, stitch the lengths together along their short ends to make one long continuously pieced strip (**B**).

If you find it difficult to work in a totally random fashion, try putting all your cut lengths in a bag or box and pull them out without looking. When I work like this, the only rule I follow is not to stitch two of the same fabrics together. I do, however, allow same fabrics to touch each other when making up the blocks. Press all the seams of the long pieced strip in the same direction.

Decide on the size of the block, then trim off sections of the continuous pieced strip to that length, plus seam allowances. Stitch all the rows together to form your block. If two seams on adjacent rows will fall in the same place when stitching the strips into blocks, re-press one of them in the opposite direction. Finally, press all the long seams of the completed block in the same direction (**C**).

Once you have made a few quilts, you will begin to accumulate the inevitable leftovers from each project. This technique is a terrific way to recycle these leftovers into scrap quilts. Make one to keep in the car, or for the kids to use in the garden.

SASHING STRIPS WITH CORNER POSTS

Dividing up sashing strips with corner posts adds a rhythmical design element to your quilt. Not only is the result attractive, it even simplifies the cutting out process. Choose a colour and value that provides a strong contrast with the fabric you have chosen for the sashing, and the squares will stand out accordingly. Alternatively, choose a fabric that is closely related in colour and value for a subtler look **(D)**. A third possibility is to use all different fabrics, perhaps utilising scraps of fabric used in the blocks.

The width of the sashing will determine the size of the square to be cut for the posts. All the long sashing strips are cut to the same length (the finished size of the block plus seam allowances), making it easy to calculate the amount of fabrics needed, and to stack and cut the strips quickly.

When stitching, sashing strips are added to the sides of the blocks. These are stitched together in the usual way to make up the block rows. The corner posts are alternated with sashing strips to make up the rows in between the block rows. When stitching the corner post rows to the block rows, pin and match the intersecting seams for accuracy.

PIECED BACKINGS

With the exception of quilt-as-you-go projects, most quilts are finished with a single fabric on the back. Yet there is no reason why you cannot have a quilt that looks a bit more interesting when it is turned over. This is also a good way to make use of smaller pieces of fabric, perhaps pieces left over from the top of the quilt. It is also a good way to deal with quilts that end up an awkward finished size, say, just a few inches or centimetres wider than a width of fabric, necessitating the purchase of a second width, most of which would then be leftover.

Any pattern can be pieced together to make a quilt backing. You may wish to echo an element used on the front, but perhaps alter the scale, or simplify it somehow. The great thing about designing a backing is the freedom from the constraints that exist when working on the "good" side.

If there is any drawback to pieced backings, it is the extra seam allowances you may have to quilt through. You can try pressing the seams open on the back to reduce the bulk, but if that isn't feasible, simply make your quilting stitches slightly larger.

"Rows of Flowers" Quilt

This pretty multi-coloured quilt echoes the
planted rows of annuals in a summer garden.
The soft pastel prints are fenced in by the green
of the sashing strips and square corner posts in
this trouble-free garden, which will give you
pleasure all year round.

Finished size: 51 x 51 in (136 x 136 cm)

MATERIALS:

Floral strips used in blocks:
16 assorted prints, ¼ yd (25 cm) each.
**Plain strips used in blocks and corner
posts:** five assorted pastel fabrics; one to
match the fabric for the sashing strips,
¼ yd (25 cm) each.
Sashing strips: green floral print fabric,
1 yd (90 cm)
Main backing: small multi-coloured
floral print, 1⅔ yds (1.5 m)
Second backing: tone-on-tone stripe,
1⅛ yds (1.1 m)
Binding: ⅔ yd (60 cm)
Wadding: 55 x 55 in (146 x 146 cm)
Rotary cutter, ruler and cutting mat
Threads: Neutral sewing thread,
hand-quilting thread
Hera marker
Fabric spray adhesive

CUTTING:

**1 From one of the floral fabrics for the
blocks, cut the following:**
● three strips 2 in (5.5 cm) deep, across the
width of the fabric. Remove the selvedges
from each strip. Stack up the three strips so
that all the edges match and cross-cut them
into two lengths of 10½ in (26.5 cm) and
three lengths of 5¾ in (14.5 cm)
(diagram 1). Set aside any scraps to use in
the blocks if long enough.

DIAGRAM 1

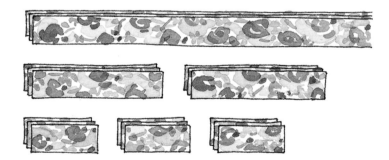

2 Repeat step 1 above for each of the
remaining fifteen floral fabrics.

**3 From the plain fabric that matches the
sashing, cut the following:**
● three strips 2 in (5.5 cm) deep, across the
width of the fabric. Remove the selvedges
from each strip. Stack up the strips as before
and cross-cut five 2 in (5.5 cm) squares, one
length of 10½ in (26.5 cm) and three lengths
of 5¾ in (14.5 cm). From the remainder of
one of the strips, cross-cut one more 2 in (5.5
cm) square to give a total of sixteen squares

QUILT PLAN

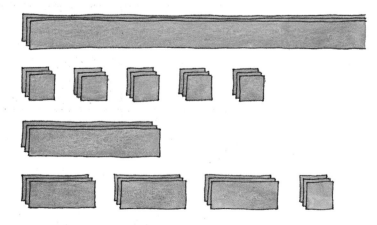

(**diagram 2**). Set these aside for the corner posts. Any remaining pieces of strip may be used in the blocks if long enough.

DIAGRAM 2

4 Cut the remaining four pastel fabrics as you did the floral ones.

5 **From the green floral print fabric for the sashing strips, cut the following:**

• twelve strips 2 in (5.5 cm) deep, across the width of the fabric. From each of these strips cut two lengths 15½ in (41.5 cm) long, avoiding the selvedges. Set these twenty-four strips aside.

6 **From the main backing fabric, cut the following:**

• three strips 18 in (48 cm) deep, across the width of the fabric. Cross-cut each strip into two 18 in (48 cm squares), avoiding the selvedges. Discard one resulting square and set the remaining five squares aside.

7 **From the second backing fabric, cut the following:**

• two strips 18 in (48 cm) deep across the width of the fabric. Cross-cut each strip into two 18 in (48 cm) squares, avoiding the selvedges. Set these four squares aside.

8 **From the binding fabric, cut the following:**

• six strips 2½ in (6 cm) deep, across the width of the fabric. Remove the selvedges from all strips and set the strips aside.

STITCHING

1 Stitch the floral and plain pastel lengths together at random to form a long continuous strip (**diagram 3**). You may find it easier to work on a few long lengths at a time, joining them all at the end.

DIAGRAM 3

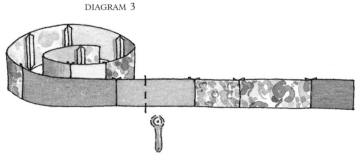

2 To make the blocks, trim the long continuous strip into shorter sections of 15½ in (41.5 cm). You will need ninety lengths, ten for each block.

3 Choose ten sections to make up a block and lay them out in front of you. If it looks like any of the short cross-seams in adjacent rows will intersect, press one of the seams in the opposite direction. Stitch the sections together in progressive pairs until the block is complete. Press the long seams in one direction. Repeat for the other eight blocks.

4 Lay your blocks out on a large, flat surface and decide on their final placement.

5 Stitch the blocks and sashing strips together into three rows of three blocks and four sashing strips each. Press all seams towards the sashing strips. Stitch the alternating rows, consisting of three sashing strips and four corner posts **(diagram 4)**. Press all seams away from the corner posts.

6 Stitch the final long seams, pinning and matching all intersecting seams.

7 Piece the large squares for the backing into what is essentially a giant nine-patch block, pressing intersecting seams on each row in alternate directions and the two final seams in the same direction.

8 Stitch the binding strips into a continuous binding.

FINISHING

1 Measure your pieced backing and cut the wadding to the same size.

2 On a large, flat surface, spread out your wadding and spray baste it according to the instructions on the spray can. Smooth the pieced backing onto the wadding, ensuring there are no wrinkles. Turn the wadding and backing over, spray baste the other side of the wadding and carefully place the quilt centrally on top of the wadding, ensuring there are no wrinkles. Place a few pins in the top for extra strength.

3 Quilt diagonally across the blocks, and outline quilt around the sashing strips **(diagram 5)**.

4 Bind the quilt with the continuous binding, mitring the corners as you go.

DIAGRAM 4

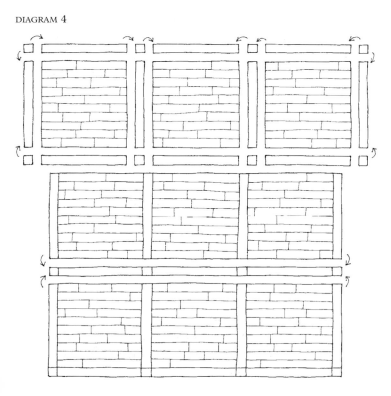

DIAGRAM 5

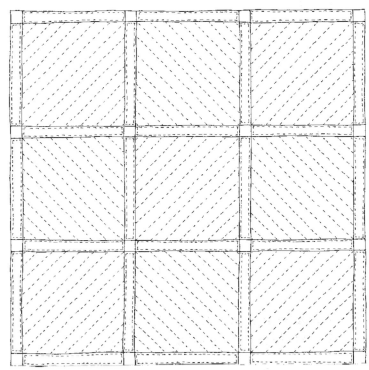

Templates

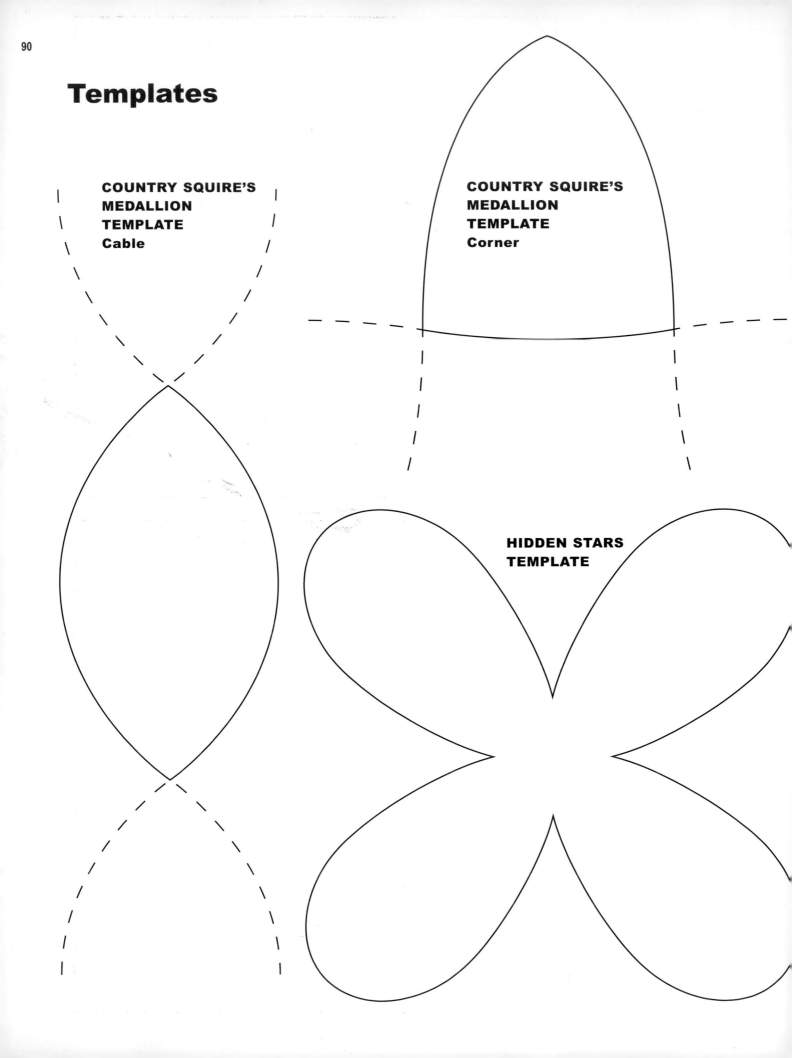

COUNTRY SQUIRE'S MEDALLION TEMPLATE
Cable

COUNTRY SQUIRE'S MEDALLION TEMPLATE
Corner

HIDDEN STARS TEMPLATE

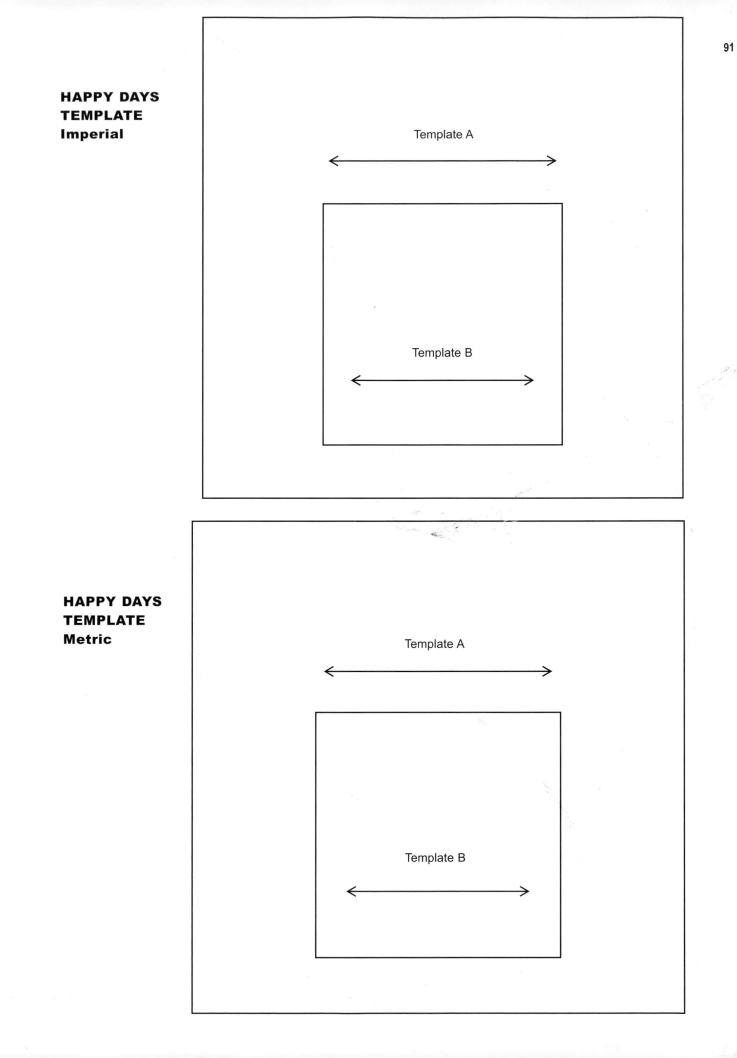

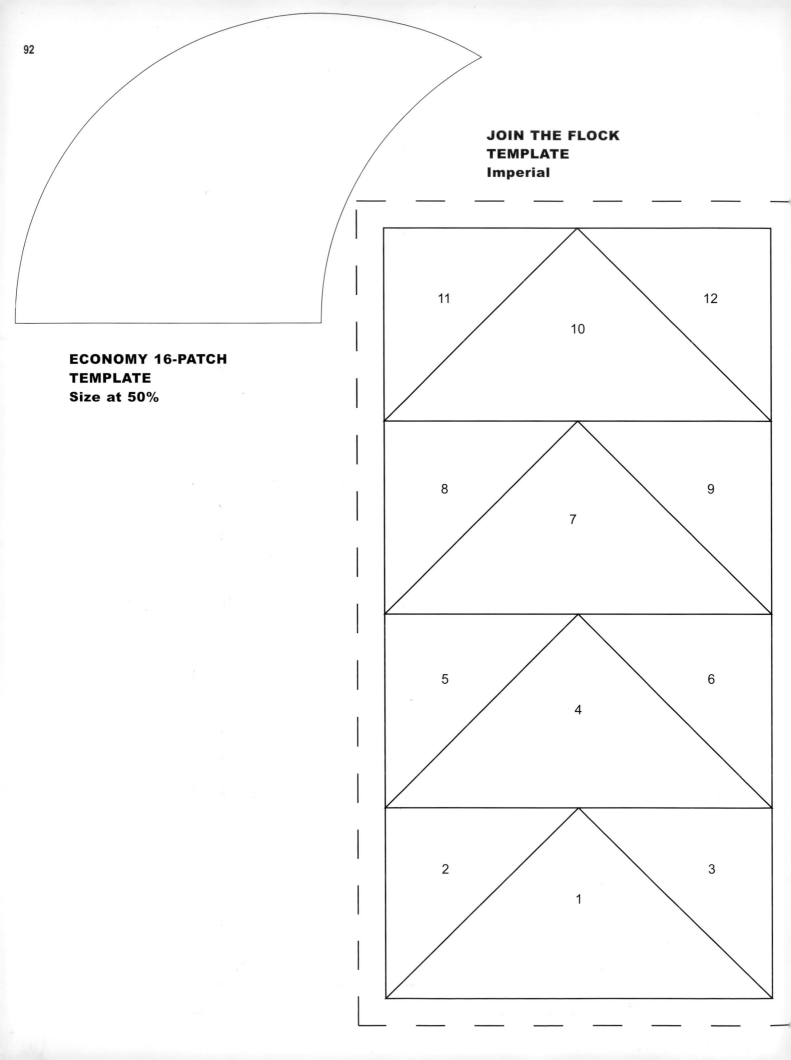

**ECONOMY 16-PATCH
TEMPLATE
Size at 50%**

**JOIN THE FLOCK
TEMPLATE
Imperial**

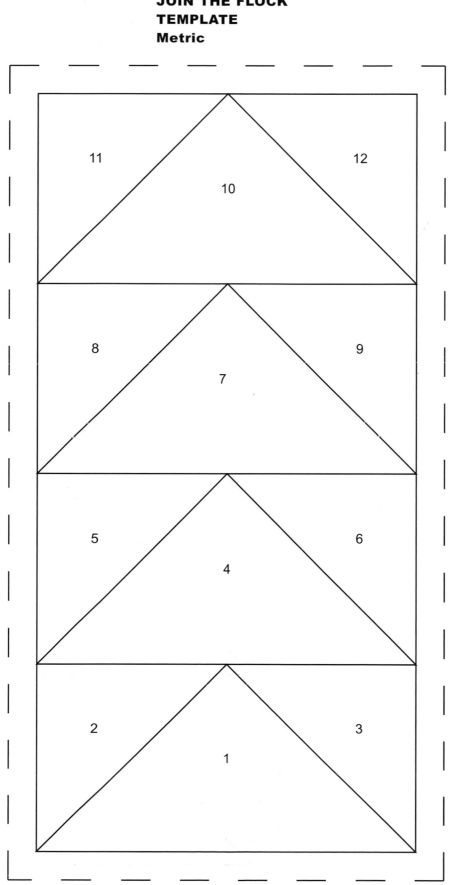

**JOIN THE FLOCK
TEMPLATE
Metric**

Suppliers

UK & Eire

Abigail Crafts
3-5 Regent Street
Stonehouse
Gloucestershire GL10
2AA
Tel: (01453) 823 691
www.abigailcrafts.co.uk
Extensive range of patchwork and embroidery supplies

The Bramble Patch
West Street
Weedon
Northants NN7 4QU
Tel: (01327) 342 212
Extensive range of patchwork and quilting supplies

Custom Quilting Limited
"Beal na Tra"
Derrymihan West
Castletownbere
Co Cork
Eire
Email: patches@iol.ie
Long arm quilting services

The Cotton Patch
1285 Stratford Road
Hall Green
Birmingham B28 9AJ
Tel: (0121) 702 2840
Extensive range of patchwork and quilting supplies

Creative Quilting
3 Bridge Road
East Molesey
Surrey KT8 9EU
Tel: (020) 8941 7075
Specialist retailer

Fabricrafts
Ferrers Centre for Arts & Crafts
Staunton Harold
Ashby-d-la-Zouch
Leicestershire
LE65 1RU
Fabric suppliers

Fred Aldous Ltd
P.O Box 135
37 Lever Street
Manchester M1 1LW
Tel: (0161) 236 2477
Mail order supplier of craft materials

Goose Chase Quilting
65 Great Norwood Street
Leckhampton
Cheltenham
GL50 2BQ
Tel: (01242) 512639
Patchwork and quilting supplies

Hab-bits
Unit 9, Vale Business Park
Cowbridge
Vale of Glamorgan
CF71 7PF
Tel: (01446) 775150
Haberdashery supplies

Patchwork Direct
c/o Heirs & Graces
King Street
Bakewell
Derbyshire DE45 1DZ
Tel: (01629) 815873
www.patchworkdirect.com
Patchwork and quilting supplies and accessories

Purely Patchwork
23 High Street
Linlithgow
West Lothian
Scotland
Tel: (01506) 846200
Patchwork and quilting supplies

Stitch in Time
293 Sandycombe Road
Kew
Surrey TW9 3LU
Tel: (020) 8948 8462
www.stitchintimeuk.com
Specialist quilting retailer

Strawberry Fayre
Chagford
Devon TQ13 8EN
Tel: (01647) 433 250
Mail order supplier of fabrics and quilts

Sunflower Fabrics
157-159 Castle Road
Bedford MK40 3RS
Tel: (01234) 273 819
www.sunflowerfabrics.co
Quilting supplies

The Quilt Loft
9/10 Havercroft Buildings
North Street
Worthing
West Sussex BN11 1DY
Tel: (01903) 233771
Quilt supplies, classes and workshops

The Quilt Room
20 West Street
Dorking
Surrey RH4 1BL
Tel: (01306) 740739
www.quiltroom.co.uk
Quilt supplies, classes and workshops
Mail order:
Tel: (01306) 87730

The Sewing Shed
Shanahill West
Keel, Castlemaine
Co Kerry
Republic of Ireland
Tel: (00353) 66 9766931
Patchwork and quilting supplies

South Africa

Crafty Supplies
Stadium on Main
Main Road
Claremont 7700
Tel: (021) 671 0286

Fern Gully
46 3rd Street
Linden
2195
Tel: (011) 782 7941

Stitch 'n' Stuff
140 Lansdowne Road
Claremont 7700
Tel: (021) 674 4059

Pied Piper
69 1st Avenue
Newton Park
Port Elizabeth 6001
Tel: (041) 365 1616

Quilt Talk
40 Victoria Street
George 6530
Tel: (044) 873 2947

Nimble Fingers
Shop 222
Kloof Village Mall
Village Road
Kloof 3610
Tel: (031) 764 6283

Quilt Tech
9 Louanna Avenue
Kloofendal
Extension 5, 1709
Tel: (011) 679 4386

Simply Stitches
2 Topaz Street
Albernarle
Germiston 1401
Tel: (011) 902 6997

Quilting Supplies
42 Nellnapius Drive
Irene 0062
Tel: (012) 667 2223

Australia

Patchwork Plus
Shop 81
7-15 Jackson Avenue
Miranda
NSW 2228
Tel: (02) 9540 278

Patchwork of Essendon
96 Fletcher Street
Essendon
VIC 3040
Tel: (03) 9372 0793

Quilts and Threads
827 Lower North East Road
Dernancourt
SA 5075
Tel: (08) 8365 6711

Riverlea Cottage Quilts
Shop 4, 330 Unley Road
Hyde Park
SA 5061
Tel: (08) 8373 0653

Country Patchwork Cottage
10/86 Erindale Road
Balcatta
WA 6021
Tel: (08) 9345 3550

The Quilters Store
22 Shaw Street
Auchenflower
QLD 4066
Tel: (07) 3870 0408

New Zealand

Patchwork Barn
132 Hinemoa Street
Birkenhead
Auckland
Tel: (09) 480 5401

Stitch and Craft
32 East Tamaki Road
Papatoetoe
Auckland
Tel: (09) 278 1351
Fax: (09) 278 1356

The Patchwork Shop
356 Grey Street
Hamilton
Tel: (07) 856 6365

The Quilt Shop
35 Pearn Place
Northcote Shopping
Centre
Auckland
Tel: (09) 480 0028
Fax: (09) 480 0380

**Grandmothers
Garden Patchwork
and Quilting**
1042 Gordonton Road
Gordonton
Hamilton
Tel: (07) 824 3050

**Needlecraft
Distributors**
600 Main Street
Palmerston North
Tel: (06) 356 4793
Fax: (06) 355 4594

**Hands Ashford Craft
Supply Store**
5 Normans Road
Christchurch
Tel: (03) 355 9099
www.hands.co.nz

Stitches
351 Colombo Street
Christchurch
Tel: (03) 379 1868
Fax: (03) 377 2347
www.stitches.co.nz

Variety Handcrafts
106 Princes Street
Dunedin
Tel: (03) 474 1088

Spotlight Stores
Whangarei (09) 430 7220
Wairau Park (09) 444
0220
Henderson (09) 836 0888
Panmure (09) 527 0915
Manukau City (09) 263
6760
Hamilton (07) 839 1793
Rotorua (07) 343 6901
New Plymouth (06) 757
3575
Gisborne (06) 863 0037
Hastings (06) 878 5223

Palmerston North (06)
357 6833
Porirua (04) 238 4055
Wellington (04) 472 5600
Christchurch (03) 377
6121
Dunedin (03) 477 1478
www.spotlight.net.nz

Index

Acknowledgements

I would like to thank the many people who have played such a large part in the production and presentation of this book, especially Clare Sayer, Steffanie Brown and Rosemary Wilkinson at New Holland. Thanks as well to all my students over the years who have made the teaching experience so enjoyable. And I owe so much to the ladies at The Quilt Room. They are more than colleagues; they are a family of friends who are constantly there with kindness, laughter, gossip, cups of tea and endless inspiration. Carolyn Forster came to my rescue and made two great quilts ("Hidden Stars", page 74, and "Economy 16-patch", page 48) with style and speed. Susie Green very kindly, and expertly, machine quilted the "Economy 16-patch" quilt at very short notice. The "Twinkling Stars" quilt, page 43, was designed and begun in a workshop tutored by Margaret Hughes. Thanks to everyone at the shop who has offered help and suggestions, but especially to Margaret Hughes, Pat Keating, Tina Lamborn and Alison Wood, the Monday and Friday teams. Thanks also to Joan Wright, a friend and faithful customer, who did a wonderful job hand-quilting the "Rows of Flowers" quilt on page 86. Finally, thanks to my quilting partners for the last twenty years, Mary Ann Corp and Mollie Edwards, who have been a constant source of inspired ideas, practical advice and far too many pastries. First, last and always, I am forever grateful to Jim, Liz and Dan for their love and encouragement, their help, their stunning ability to ignore chaos and their way of making me laugh even when I don't want to.